GOSPEL POWER

MAGNIFIED

THROUGH HUMAN WEAKNESS

Nelson D. Kloosterman

Reformed Fellowship
4855 Starr Street S.E.
Grand Rapids, MI 49546
USA

TABLE OF CONTENTS

GOSPEL POWER

MAGNIFIED

THROUGH HUMAN WEAKNESS

INTRODUCTION

In the church, of all communities, people should understand human weakness most sympathetically. For in the church, divine strength has embraced, and transformed, human weakness. This gospel reminds us perpetually of both our sin and our feebleness, so that we may learn to deal effectively with those of others.

Yet, it seems today that many *church members* are embarrassed by ordinary weakness. 'Power' diets and 'power' sales methods need to be matched by a 'power' religion. In our day (as in Paul's) some demand a sign, while others seek the power of knowledge (see 1 Cor. 1:21-25). In our age of splash and dash, fewer church people seem willing to put up with mediocre preachers or church members, with plodding but faithful sermons, and with ordinary worship services. Their solution is to make religion and the church attractive, with the help of silk-tongued rhetoricians, scintillating music, and seekers' services. But with these and similar 'solutions,' the Christian religion is in danger of becoming just another 'attraction,' like the county fair sideshow and the state basketball tournament. Boredom within religion may be the curse of our age.

As the remedy for ecclesiastical boredom and the antidote to the longing for a socially and culturally 'impressive' religion, the epistle of 2 Corinthians extols *gospel power magnified through human weakness.* In this letter, the apostle Paul uses emotional appeals laced with red-hot irony, and pastoral diplomacy guided by winsome logic. He aims to guide the young Corinthian congregation away from her penchant for measuring the church's life and leadership by human standards. At stake, really, is the gospel message itself: its core consists of the cross of Jesus Christ as history's decisive show of divine power magnified in human weakness. *Because* the cross is an emblem of shame and suffering, it is also *the* symbol of victory and power.

So the congregation must be called to demonstrate the gospel preeminently in her style and in her expectations of pastoral leadership.

May God use these studies to help you, whether pastor or pew-sitter, whether standing on the front line or squeezed in the middle of the pack, to fashion your church-style by the style of the gospel.

Nelson D. Kloosterman
Summer, 1992

LITERATURE

For most people, the epistle of 2 Corinthians is an unfamiliar and challenging letter. Perhaps these helpful commentaries can be obtained for your personal and church libraries:

From Triumphalism to Maturity: An Exposition of 2 Corinthians 10-13, Donald A. Carson (Grand Rapids, MI: Baker Book House, 1984).

An Exposition of the Second Epistle to the Corinthians, Charles Hodge (Grand Rapids, MI: Eerdmans, 1950).

Paul's Second Epistle to the Corinthians, by Philip E. Hughes (New International Commentary on the New Testament; Grand Rapids, MI: Eerdmans, 1962).

2 Corinthians, by Aída Besançon Spencer and William David Spencer (Bible Study Commentary; Grand Rapids, MI: Zondervan Publishing House, 1989).

Lesson 1

2 Corinthians 1:1-2:2

Ministerial Comfort and Constancy

Memory Verse: 'For all the promises of God in [Jesus Christ] are Yes, and in Him Amen, to the glory of God through us. Now He who establishes us with you in Christ and has anointed us is God, who also has sealed us and given us the Spirit in our hearts as a deposit.'

2 Corinthians 1:20-22

Paul and the Corinthians

Paul's pastoral relationship with the Corinthians spans a seven-year period. He spent a year and a half in Corinth establishing the church (see Acts 18:1-18, 18:27-19:1). This was followed some four or five years later with a second visit, a painful visit, where he dealt with an unknown disciplinary problem in the congregation. About a year later, Paul stayed for the third time in Corinth, for about three months (13:1).

Of all the churches which this apostle pastored, the congregation in Corinth was perhaps the most demanding. From 1 Corinthians we learn that the church was afflicted with problems ranging from divisions, immorality, and lawsuits, to doubts about the resurrection. From 2 Corinthians we detect that severe criticisms were being leveled in the congregation against Paul's person and ministry.

We might summarize the purpose of this letter as being to prepare the Corinthian believers for his impending visit, to defend himself against growing criticism, to urge the congregation to band together in Christian service, and to exhort these church members to repentance and maturity in Christ.

The apostle's greeting sets the tone (read 1:1-2)

Identifying himself as one sent out on behalf of Jesus Christ, not by his own initiative, but by the will of God Himself, the apostle Paul lays down his credentials, as it were. What he is about to write must be read not as the blustering of someone irritated by criticism. No, Paul writes in the name of his Sender! Others may pretend to be apostles (see 11:13), but Paul was met and separated for service on the Damascus road by Christ Himself.

Though nowhere called an 'apostle' in the New Testament, Timothy was Paul's spiritual son and frequent missionary companion. He joined in sending this letter not only to believers in Corinth, but to those living in the province of Achaia as well. Copies of this epistle were probably made and distributed among churches in this region and beyond. This reminds us that when the Holy Spirit inspired this letter, the apostle expected it to be read in churches other than the one addressed (see Col. 4:16). Paul writes to 'the church *of God*' in Corinth—not Paul, but *God*, owns the church, purchased with the blood of His own dear Son (see Acts 20:28). This too sets the tone for what Paul is going to write in his own defense, and in pastoral encouragement and exhortation.

Notice carefully Paul's apostolic declaration: 'Grace to you and peace from God our Father and the Lord Jesus Christ.' Peace (harmonious fellowship with both God and man) depends on grace (undeserved favor earned by the Lord Jesus Christ, the basis of forgiveness); both of these components belong to that divinely provided reconciliation of which Paul is the privileged preacher.

This, then, sets the pastoral tone of 2 Corinthians, an epistle full of authorized counsel to God's people, a tone and content dependent on Christ's finished and continuing work of redemption. (*Question 1*)

Blessed be God our Comforter (read 1:3-7)

As you read 1:3-7, the single word too prominent to miss is 'comfort.' As he so often begins his epistles, here too the apostle follows his greeting with a beatitude, a prayer, so uplifting and thrilling!

Our attention is immediately drawn to the character and beauty of God, who is described in three important ways: as 'the God and Father of our Lord Jesus Christ,' as 'the Father of mercies,' and as 'God of all comfort.' This sequence of descriptions yields a portrait of divine and human consolation. As the source of *all* comfort, God stood alongside Paul and Timothy in their missionary and pastoral labors (the 'we,' 'us' and 'our' of verses 4-7 refer to them, *not* to the Corinthian believers).

10

Divine comfort enables Paul and Timothy to comfort others in trouble, since God's comfort is the source of all pastoral consolation.

Moreover, since believers are united by faith with Christ, His sufferings become their sufferings. These are not the afflictions that befall every member of the human race, but are rather tribulations suffered for Christ's sake. Persecution for the sake of principle, rejection on account of religion, hardship because of self-denial—have you met any of these? If not, read 2 Timothy 3:12 before continuing.

The Lord Jesus Christ is also the Mediator of comfort (verse 5b). For every tear, He provides a towel, so to speak. Old Testament Israel received the promise that 'As one whom his mother comforts, so I will comfort you; and you shall be comforted in Jerusalem' (Isa. 66:13). The gospel's power is experienced personally as divine comfort *during* tribulation. Here on earth, God's peace doesn't necessarily remove pain, but it tempers and sanctifies our tears. So optimistic about this is the apostle, that he declares as his firm hope that those in the Corinthian church who are faithful will receive God's consolation commensurate with their suffering for Christ's sake. (*Questions 2 and 3*)

Blessed be God our Deliverer (read 1:8-11)

The afflictions of the previous paragraph are now expanded upon. Somewhere in Asia (likely Ephesus), Paul had endured hardships so severe that they weighed him down 'beyond measure,' causing him to despair of life itself. Indeed, this tribulation involved 'the sentence of death' (whether a literal verdict or a figurative description, we cannot be sure), bringing Paul to his wits' end, confronting him with the need to trust in God alone for his deliverance.

Here again we meet the epistle's theme: facing the limit of his endurance, overwhelmed with oppression, Paul is delivered by 'God who raises the dead.' So amazing is this deliverance that he describes it in past, present and future tenses (verse 10). This is the God whose *name* is 'Deliverance'! For God's child, resurrection is virtually a daily occurrence.

As Deliverer, God is personally responsive to the Corinthians' faith and prayer (verse 11). This exercise of congregational supplication (prayer for others) is but the prelude to congregational thanksgiving. Both are rooted in a profound trust in the power and goodness of God.

Pastoral constancy during a change of plans (read 1:12-2:2)

From verses 12 and 17 we surmise that some within the Corinthian congregation were criticizing Paul for improper pastoral conduct, improper before the world and the church. His sincerity and consistency were being questioned, because he had changed his travel plans. Originally the apostle had planned to travel from Ephesus to Corinth, on to Macedonia, and then back to Corinth ('a second benefit,' 1:15-16). But circumstances arose that required Paul to revise his plans, so that he would be traveling from Ephesus to Troas, into Macedonia and south to Corinth (1 Cor. 16:5-7). This change was seized upon by his opponents in the congregation who argued that, since Paul's word was unreliable, so were his character and his message. (*Question 4*)

So by means of two rhetorical questions (verse 17), Paul intends to deny that his original purpose was made lightly and that his plans were governed by worldly or fleshly considerations. Rather, his intention was pastoral love (see verse 23).

The heart of the problem, however, involves more than change of itinerary. At stake is the reliability of God Himself, whose messenger Paul has become. The apostle's critics had been mildly successful in getting a finger behind Paul's message, his gospel of salvation by grace through faith in the Lord Jesus Christ. The apostle realized that if *his* 'Yes' also means 'No,' if his word was really infected with ambiguity, then the same would be true of *God's* Word and promises. God's Word too, by extension of the argument, must be infected with the ambiguity of yes-*and*-no, of do-*and*-don't, in the same breath! Notice how, in verses 19-22, the apostle brings the 'issue' to focus in Jesus Christ. He alone is the 'Amen' of all God's promises! This Jesus Christ is the One who authenticates His own teaching, having no need of another witness, when He said, 'Amen, amen, *I* say to you. . . .' This word 'Amen' conveys the idea of firmness and reliability; our 'Amen' is the voice of faith setting its seal that God is true (see John 3:33).

We learn from verses 21-22 of several divine activities that authenticate the reliability and integrity of the apostle and his word. First, God establishes (present tense) Paul, along with the Corinthian believers, in Christ. Second, the Lord has anointed (past tense) Paul, which anointing is further certification of Paul's sincerity and trustworthiness. Third, the apostle has been sealed with God's own Spirit, enjoying thereby the twin benefits of identification with God and protection by Him. This Holy Spirit has been given, fourthly, as the internal, good-faith down-payment on full redemption. How incongruous, therefore, for such an apostle, one in whom and upon whom the Triune God has worked and is working, to lack sincerity and integrity toward the Corinthians!

Since Paul is seeking to affirm his own integrity in this passage, these verses refer explicitly to the apostle (who frequently employs 'we' and 'us' for himself, see verses 8ff., 15ff., 23f.). But that is not their exclusive application. Because he identifies himself with the Corinthian believers, the divine activities enumerated belong to all believers as well. God renders *all His people* firm and secure in their union with Christ, and makes them share in the benefits of redemption, through the work of His indwelling Spirit. All of this has become effectual through Paul's apostolic word of preaching—which has been under attack within the congregation. So, then, part of the evidence disproving these charges consists in the continuing sanctification of believers in Corinth! Christ's working Word, proclaimed by Paul, certifies his reliability. (*Question 5*)

In verses 23-24 the apostle summons God Himself as witness to his sincerity of motive. His 'philosophy of ministry' was openness (not pretense), cooperation (not domination), God-centeredness (not self-centeredness).

We learn more from 2:1-2 about Paul's motives for changing his travel plans. He had paid an emergency visit to Corinth earlier, to correct abuses in the congregation (see 12:14 and 13:1f.). Paul did not wish to have another 'painful visit,' but instead to await word from Titus about the effect of his letter. From 7:8-9 we discover that its effect was positive: the congregation in Corinth had repented! So deep is the apostle's affection for the Corinthians that their sorrow was his sorrow (2:2). If they were not happy, he could not be happy. In his change of plans, therefore, there was no hint of irresoluteness or irresponsibility, but a desire for their spiritual joy and well-being.

Questions for Reflection and Reply

1. Paul's commission and authority came 'by the will of God,' not by 'the will of man' (see Gal. 1:1). What does it mean that someone becomes a minister by 'the will of man'? Why would someone enter the ministry based on 'the will of man'? How would this affect pastoral practice?

2. Read 1 Cor. 1:4. Often God does not comfort His children by removing their trial, but by strengthening them to endure it. Why? Can unbelievers be truly comforted?

3. Read 1 Cor. 1:7. Mention examples of suffering for Christ's sake in your life. Explain in personal terms how Christ's comfort sustains you in these tribulations.

4. Why do some people seem to enjoy criticizing their spiritual leaders? How must we in the church distinguish a trivial criticism from an important complaint?

5. In the light of Eph. 1:13-14 and 4:30, along with 2 Cor. 1:22, when are believers anointed, sealed and given the Holy Spirit as a down-payment? What does it mean to be 'sealed'? By what means are believers and their children sealed?

Lesson 2

2 Corinthians 2:3-17

Pastoral Tenderness Serving the Gospel's Triumph

Memory Verse: 'Now thanks be to God who always leads us in triumph
in Christ, and through us diffuses the fragrance of His
knowledge in every place. For we are to God the
fragrance of Christ among those who are being saved
and among those who are perishing.'

2 Corinthians 2:14-15

Gospel power threatened by harsh church discipline (read 2:3-11)

As with so many passages in Paul's letters, this one too draws us
near to the apostle's pastoral heart. Writing to his spiritual children in
Corinth of his sorrow and joy, of his forgiveness and love, he aims his
affection from his heart to theirs.

In verse 3 Paul refers to a letter he had written earlier (very likely 1
Corinthians), in which he had rebuked them sharply for tolerating sin
in the church. There had been a moral offender within the congregation who had required the love of discipline to bring him back to the
Lord, but the Corinthians had not provided it. Historically interpreters
have identified this offender as the one mentioned in 1 Corinthians 5.
Despite Paul's former admonitions, here in this second epistle he
declares his confidence in all of them, without exception, a confidence
that his joy is their joy.

This pastor's heart opens wide in verse 4, where he piles phrase
upon phrase to describe the condition in which he wrote his earlier
epistle: his heart had ached with affliction and anguish for them, his
eyes had brimmed with tears as he thought of them. But his twofold
purpose in writing them had remained steadfast: negatively, that they
should not be grieved; positively, that they might comprehend his
overflowing love for them. Like any sensitive parent, he knew that the
one most pained by this whole experience was not Paul himself, but the
Corinthian congregation, since everyone had been affected to some

extent by the sin, by his consequent rebuke, and by the discipline. (*Question 1*)

But now their discipline had gone on long enough. The sinner had repented, and such repentance must be met with tender forgiveness, not persisting punishment. The unintended effect of such discipline may be that the sinner despairs of grace and is overcome with hopeless sorrow for his sin. Undue severity in discipline is to be avoided as much as undue leniency. Our God Himself provides the pattern for discipline, in His fierce denunciation of impenitence and tender embrace of all who acknowledge their sins and turn to Him. 'A bruised reed He will not break, and smoking flax He will not quench' (Isa. 42:3). (*Question 2*)

So the apostle calls upon the congregation to reinstate the penitent offender in the communion. Paul himself is ready to join in extending that forgiveness (verse 10). As an added motive to follow his advice, the apostle points to the danger of Satan taking advantage of something so good as church discipline. 'We know his devices,' writes the apostle, suggesting that especially in the church, believers must be on guard that Satan does not pervert our practices of religious devotion and holiness. (*Question 3*)

Gospel triumph through its double effect (read 2:12-16)

Shortly after dispatching his earlier letter to Corinth, Paul had gone to Troas on a preaching mission. There he was awaiting news from his co-worker Titus, who had visited Corinth and was expected to bring back a report on the effect of Paul's letter among the congregation. Suffering turmoil in spirit because of his concern for the Corinthians, and after waiting in vain for Titus, Paul traveled to Macedonia, where he met his fellow worker and heard his encouraging report of their godly submission to the apostle's instruction (see 7:5ff., where this discussion is resumed).

Quite characteristically, the apostle breaks off into one of his rich digressions, breaking forth into exuberant thanksgiving about the power of the gospel of Jesus Christ. So encouraged was he by the report that Titus brought!

He expresses his gratitude with a metaphor. Paul pictures himself walking in a triumphal procession, led by God the victorious General, as it were. This triumph, let it be clear, is only 'in Christ,' that is: enjoyed and extended through union with Him. But those walking in the parade, in good Roman style, were conquered enemies who had become slaves of the Victor! Paul and his associates knew themselves to be slaves of the Lord Jesus Christ, slaves who, strangely enough, were at the same time fellow-victors with Him!

Associated with this victory march was the release of sweet-smelling odors from burning spices used to add festivity to the parade. Now, it is important to notice that in this particular victory march, the fragrance has a twofold identity. In *people's* nostrils, it consists of 'the fragrance of His [Christ's] knowledge in every place,' a universal odor diffused or spread by those proclaiming His name (see verse 14, 'through us'). And in *God's* nostrils, the fragrance is the messengers themselves (verse 15a). In both cases, Christ is the source of its sweetness. This odor is sweet-smelling *to God*, as it is spread among both those being saved (believers) and those perishing (unbelievers). This latter is important: even when grace is rejected, it does not cease to be grace! Though its effect will be the condemnation of all who reject it, the fragrance will nevertheless be sweet-smelling to God. It remains the 'fragrance of Christ'!

The effects of this spreading fragrance are twofold, and antithetical. For those who reject the message of reconciliation, the result is death. But it is life to those who by God's Spirit receive it with obedient faith. Gospel preaching *is* power! Sermons *do* something! They lead one to either life or death. But we must remember what Calvin said, namely, that the proper purpose of gospel preaching is salvation, while its 'accidental' (that is, non-essential) function is death, which must always be imputed to human depravity. If some are saved, to God belongs the glory; but if some are lost, to them belongs the blame! (*Questions 4 and 5*)

Pastoral sincerity despite insufficiency (read 2:17)

Paul realizes the burdensome connection between the message and the man bringing it. The gates of heaven and hell are opened by this preaching! 'Who is sufficient for these things?' he cries out in humble admission of his own inadequacy. Who is 'up to' this kind of responsibility, with this kind of result? No mere man, that's for sure. Later, in 3:5, he answers his own question: 'Not that we are sufficient of ourselves to think of anything as being from ourselves, but our sufficiency is from God.'

For the first time in this epistle Paul mentions his opponents directly. Placing his own ministry alongside theirs, he compares them on the level of ministerial practice. 'So many,' complains the apostle, '*peddle* the word of God.' They hawk it like paste jewelry or cheap insurance. They're not interested first in the gospel's content, or in the congregation, or in acquitting themselves of a divine commission. Later (11:4) he will complain that they proclaim a different Jesus and another gospel. These false apostles, or pastors of pretense, have exchanged their calling for a profession, being hirelings rather than true shepherds, seeking the social and economic benefits accruing to their position. Their 'ministry' is characterized by manipulation and selfishness. Everything about them—their message, methods and motives—detracts from the gospel of Jesus Christ. Unlike them, Paul and his co-workers bring God's Word sincerely, spiritually ('as from God'), and responsibly ('in the sight of God in Christ'). They are constantly aware that their commission is from God, and that they are accountable to Him for their fulfillment of that assignment. (*Question 6*)

Here, then, we find in a nutshell Paul's explanation of his pastoral method. He will return to this matter later in the epistle. But we must see the glorious task assigned to all who preach God's Word, men who in themselves are inadequate and ill-equipped, yet men whom the Lord sovereignly uses in His service and strengthens for His purposes.

Questions for Reflection and Reply

1. Read Hebrews 12:7-17. Explain why refusing to discipline impenitent sinners (whether in family, school, church, or society) reflects the *lack* of love. What do people mean today by the phrase 'tough love'?

2. How must we determine when enough discipline has been administered? Explain why stopping discipline too soon is just as dangerous as carrying it out too long.

3. Explain how Satan can pervert and take advantage of church discipline. Why does the discipline offered by the cults seem more attractive to some people than the church's discipline?

4. Explain why the rejection of divine grace does *not* mean that grace has failed. Consider in your answer the following testimony:

   'Moreover, Holy Scripture most especially highlights this eternal and undeserved *grace* of our election and brings it out more clearly for us, in that it further bears witness that not all people have been chosen but that some have not been chosen or have been passed by in God's eternal election . . .' (*Canons of Dort*, Chapter 1, Article 15).

How is divine *grace* highlighted by the passing by and reprobation of some unto eternal death?

5. If sermons open the gates of heaven and hell, how should this truth affect preaching and public worship?

6. As in Paul's day, there are some today who 'peddle God's Word.' How can we distinguish those who are sincere servants of God's Word from those who 'peddle' it for personal profit and glory? Illustrate how the *message*, *methods* and *motives* of the modern religious 'peddler' differ from those of the sincere servant.

Lesson 3

2 Corinthians 3:1-18

The Surpassing Excellence of the New Covenant

Memory Verse: 'But we all, with unveiled face, beholding as in a mirror the glory of the Lord, are being transformed into the same image from glory to glory, just as by the Spirit of the Lord.'

2 Corinthians 3:18

Living credentials of a faithful ministry (read 3:1-3)

Although the apostle had affirmed his own sincerity in the face of religious peddlers, he realizes that his opponents in Corinth would be twisting his words into evidence of self-centeredness. So he forestalls these critics by anticipating their charge.

These people Paul portrays as intruders who have been able to enter the Corinthian congregation on the basis of certain letters of commendation. It was customary, even necessary, in the early church for traveling preachers like Paul and his co-workers to have such letters. For the region was full of charlatans who tried to live off the churches as itinerant teachers. These letters, then, were needed for entering as well as leaving a particular place (letters 'to you' and 'from you'). On other occasions, Paul himself had furnished such letters for Phoebe (Rom. 16:1ff.) and Barnabas (Col. 4:10).

But unlike someone who came around waving a letter in his hand or carrying it in his briefcase, Paul had a letter of commendation far more intimate and far more permanent than a piece of paper. This letter consisted of nothing less than transformed lives. The congregation itself composed this letter! Transformed fornicators, homosexuals, thieves and drunkards (see 1 Cor. 6:11), changed by the power of the gospel, provide indisputable evidence of the genuineness of Paul's apostolicity. This 'letter' Paul carried around in his heart, that center of pastoral love and devotion. (*Question 1*)

The church in Corinth was an 'open letter,' legible to everybody.

The Author was Christ Himself (notice the apostle's humility: not *he*, but *Christ*, gets credit for these transformed lives). Paul and his associates were merely the pen by which the Holy Spirit wrote. This Spirit is 'of the living God'; what He wrote is both intimately alive and permanently engraved.

Moreover, the writing material used by the Spirit was not stone tablets, but human hearts. Here the apostle compares the old and new dispensations or administrations of God's covenant of grace. The first was external, given on Mount Sinai, written by God's own finger. The second was internal, brought into being by the Holy Spirit within the human personality. Both Jeremiah (31:33) and Ezekiel (11:19 and 36:26) had prophesied this 'inscripturation' of God's will. Paul is *not finding fault* with the old dispensation, for the believer is still under obligation to keep the law of God. The notion that the Old Testament presents an essentially different way of salvation, or faith-demands that are essentially different than those the New Testament proclaims, is quite mistaken and spiritually destructive. Neither God nor His law changes. But there is indeed a difference between these two administrations of grace, and that vital difference is this: the believer now has the *power* of Christ, by the Holy Spirit, *within* himself, to keep God's commandments. Here is the surpassing excellence of the new covenant, which becomes the 'letter of commendation' upon Paul's ministry in Corinth!

In regard to our attitude toward the 'old covenant' there are two equally dangerous positions being advocated today. One is to say that the Old Testament is not relevant to the Christian, since we are no longer under law, but under grace. The other mistake being made today is to say that Christ intended all of the Old Testament legislation—*especially the civil laws*—to be employed directly for modern social and political life.

We cannot deal adequately here with both of these mistakes. But we must see that they both arise from a misunderstanding of the relation between the two testaments. Those who dismiss the Old Testament overemphasize the *discontinuity* between Old from New, while those who wish to enforce Old Testament laws place the wrong stress on the *continuity* between Old with New. To the first, we must say that although the ceremonies and types are all fulfilled ('blossomed') in Jesus Christ, their spiritual truth must guide us today, through the light of New Testament teaching. Those who want to employ Old Testament theocratic legislation as modern public policy need to see that the form of the old dispensation was one of immaturity, incompetence and externality, whose 'bud' has blossomed full-flowered in Jesus Christ. We who live on this side of Good Friday, Easter, Ascension and Pentecost must therefore refuse to be brought again into bondage to that old form of covenant administration (Gal. 3:19-25; 4:9-10). (*Question 2*)

God-given confidence for a competent ministry (read 3:4-6)

With such a 'letter' to serve as his recommendation, the apostle has good reason for confidence. In genuine humility, he confesses God as the source of his confidence, and Christ as the mediator thereof. Here again we meet the theme of this epistle, namely, that divine grace is exalted through human weakness.

What generates this confidence? Certainly not trust in his own abilities! Rather, this pastoral sufficiency comes from looking at the nature of the administration of the new covenant.

Paul compares the ministry of the *old* covenant with that of the *new*, describing the former as a ministry 'of the letter' that kills, and the latter the ministry 'of the Spirit' who gives life. The way in which God dealt with the Old Testament church is inferior to the way He relates to the New Testament church. The letter (or law) is inferior to the Spirit.

Remember, however, that other biblical passages (even of Paul) remind us that God's law is holy and good (see Rom. 7:10ff.), and that the Old Testament requirement of righteousness, measured by that law, was just (see Rom. 10:5; Gal. 3:12). Be careful also to avoid the notion that Paul is playing off 'letter' against 'spirit,' as if the 'spirit' refers to 'deeper (spiritual) intent' and the 'letter' to no more than outward form. Occasionally you'll hear people justify breaking God's law by saying that while they may not have kept the 'letter' of the law, they certainly honored its 'spirit.' This kind of reasoning breeds disrespect for God's Word (also called 'antinomianism,' being against law).

The contrast is rather between the external, death-dealing function of the law in its exposure of sin, and the internal, power-giving Spirit of God who enables us to make a small beginning in obedience.

The glory of Moses and the glory of Christ (read 3:7-18)

Still, the apostle must confront more forcefully his 'back-to-Moses' opponents. His covenant-comparison continues.

There was no doubt in Paul's mind about the *glory* of the old dispensation. So glorious was the LORD of Israel that Moses' face shone too brightly for eyes to behold (Ex. 34:29-30). And yet that shining glory—just like the dispensation it represented—*was temporary!*

Moreover, the *effects* of the two covenant administrations are markedly different. The first was 'the ministry of condemnation'; the law could surely diagnose spiritual ills, but was impotent in suggesting a remedy for them. To all men, the law's last word is: GUILTY! But the second, fuller covenant administration was 'the ministry of righteousness,' that is: it provided righteousness through a Mediator who fulfilled the law's demands. To those who believe in Jesus Christ the Righteous One, its last word is: ACQUITTED!

So breathtaking is this difference that one can hardly find words to describe the comparison. Scripture says, as it were, 'If the old covenant was glorious, with all its external trappings (and it was: have you ever been to Jerusalem's temple during high feast days?!), it had a temporary glory. Its magnificence was *nothing* compared to the glory of the new covenant. In terms of its power and glory, the old alongside the new is like a candle next to the sun!' (*Question 3*)

Now, let's not lose the apostle's point: he returns in verse 12 to the matter of his ministerial confidence, when he writes, 'Therefore, since we have such hope, we use great boldness of speech— . . . .' *Hope . . . boldness.* The gospel's glory is an abiding and permanent glory. What's coming in the new heavens and the new earth isn't something 'other,' but only something 'more' than what we New Testament believers *already* enjoy. This confidence permits apostolic and pastoral courage, an open ministry, aggressively countering Satan's attacks and turning back every lie and wickedness.

Moses' ministry, by contrast, was less open. From Exodus 34:32ff., we learn that Moses was in the habit, when he had finished speaking to Israel, of putting a veil over his face (Ex. 34:33). Even though God's glory was reflected and temporary on Moses' face, the sinful Israelites could not look upon that splendor. Moses covered his face, not so much for the convenience of the people, but as a kind of parable demonstrating that it was their sin that rendered them unable and unworthy to behold God's glory. The veiling of Moses' face was a condemnation of the people. The interruption and concealing of God's glory was required by the presence of human sin. *And this characterized the entire old covenant administration. It had always ended up showing a person only his guilt!*

By contrast, Paul's ministry—and that of every New Testament pastor!—is to be marked by the message of grace and mercy to every sinner who repents and believes in the Lord Jesus Christ, of holiness in Christ, of victory through His blood.

For those who refuse to believe in Jesus of Nazareth as Messiah, the veil covering Moses' *face* has become a veil covering Moses' *book*, the Old Testament (verses 14-16). The condemnation symbolized becomes judgment internalized! This veil is a hardness of heart in the face of glorious revelation. Christ-rejecting Jews cannot understand 'their' Moses, as the Master Himself said to the Moses-experts: 'For if you believed Moses, you would believe me; for he wrote about me. But if you do not believe his writings, how will you believe my words?' (John 5:46-47). This veil is lifted only when one turns to the Lord (3:16). *Conversion, not legislation, is the way life is administered in the new covenant.* (*Question 4*)

Recognizing this Jesus Christ as Lord of Israel is the key to understanding the Old Testament. In saying that 'the Lord is the Spirit,' the apostle is emphasizing not that Christ and the Spirit are the same *person*, but that they are indeed the same *being*, in the same sense in which Christ says 'I and my Father are one' (John 10:30). This identity of Christ and the Holy Spirit is important for the correct reading of Scripture (see verses 14-16). By turning unto Christ, we become partakers of the Holy Spirit, and of the liberty that flows from His application of Christ's work to us. This liberty includes freedom from the curse and penalty of the law, from the power and dominion of sin, and from the darkness of unbelief.

This characteristic openness and freedom of the ministry of the new covenant the apostle now applies to New Testament believers. *Moses* wore a veil over his face; *unbelieving Jews* wear a veil over their hearts. But the *church* has the veil removed—notice: *we* (plural) behold with unveiled *face* (singular). Hers is the privilege of seeing the glory of the Lord Jesus Christ, her approaching Bridegroom (see John 1:14,18). Moreover, we see His glory (Him!) as in a mirror, reflected in the life-giving gospel administered within His blood-bought, Spirit-invigorated congregation.

And the longer we look at this Christ-generated congregational glory, the more we are being changed into the image of God in Christ Jesus, increasingly so ('from glory to glory'). In contrast to Moses' glory, Christ's is unfading and uninterrupted, always increasing in the lives of His followers. He brings us back, beyond Sinai, to Paradise, where God's image in man was defaced by sin. The restoration or repair of this image of God is the goal of Christ's redemption and of the Spirit's application thereof, expressed elsewhere as 'the measure of the stature of the fullness of Christ' (Eph. 4:13). Our Christ-likeness is the glory-ous aim of the Spirit—and of all His new covenant ministers! (*Question 5*)

24

Questions for Reflection and Reply

1. Paul appeals to transformed lives as evidence proving the genuineness of his message. What are some other kinds of 'evidence' people look for? Why can't numerical growth be used to prove the Scriptural nature of a church's ministry?

2. Why would some believers be inclined to *dismiss* the Old Testament civil laws as irrelevant? Why would others want to *enforce* them in modern society? What are some results of each view that are quite dangerous for the church?

3. Read Hebrews 11:39. Mention several reasons why believers living after Christ 'have it better' than those living before Christ.

4. 'Conversion, not legislation, is the way life is administered in the new covenant.' What is conversion (see *Heidelberg Catechism*, Lord's Day 33, or *Westminster Confession of Faith*, Ch. XV)? Describe sermons that emphasize conversion rather than legislation. Why must we continually hear preaching that emphasizes conversion? How often must we be converted? How does 'preaching for the listener's conversion' relate to so-called 'covenantal preaching'?

5. Notice that 2 Corinthians 3 ends by emphasizing transformed lives. No church, no Christian, can maintain the status quo, or 'the way things are.' Change is inevitable, whether for better or for worse. How can Christians pursue daily transformation for the better? Mention some areas in which you have changed for the better in the last month. Write down some thoughts about the process of change—who helped you? how long did it take? what resources were useful?

Lesson 4

2 Corinthians 4:1-18

The Gospel's Glory Sustains its Frail Messengers

Memory Verse: 'For we do not preach ourselves, but Christ Jesus the Lord, and ourselves your servants for Jesus' sake. For it is the God who commanded light to shine out of darkness who has shone in our hearts to give the light of the knowledge of the glory of God in the face of Jesus Christ.'

2 Corinthians 4:5-6

Ministry methods suited to gospel glory (read 4:1-6)

The ministry of the new covenant is a ministry of life and power, of righteousness and freedom. Paul has this calling, not by his own achievement, but by virtue of divine mercy. 'Mercy' is one of those 'Bible words' we need to know well. Mercy presumes guilt, misery and unworthiness. As a recipient of mercy, the apostle's humble confidence in ministering the new covenant gospel arises in connection with his personal experience of both the law's crushing judgment and Christ's reviving grace.

The method of gospel ministry is also determined by the glorious openness and power that we studied in our last lesson on 2 Corinthians 3.

For when Paul received, on the Damascus road, God's mercy and Christ's call, he also renounced those shameful things done in secret. He refused, then and there, to deal with people through trickery. Nor would he use God's Word deceitfully, manipulating others out of self-interest. By implication, his Corinthian opponents, false apostles with a judaizing message (urging return to old covenant style), were employing craft and dishonesty in twisting Paul's words and subverting the congregation.

Paul had no use for underhandedness in this ministry of glory. In fact, by declaring openly and consistently the Word of God, the apostle confidently invites the judgment of anybody's conscience upon his ministry. His confident openness resulted from carrying on his work 'in the sight of God' (verse 2). Paul could entrust himself to human consciences because he knew of the higher scrutiny his work had received. He knew that it was to God that every minister has to answer, finally and eternally. (*Question 1*)

From verse 3 we learn that some had perhaps pointed to the ineffectiveness of Paul's ministry as proof of its deficiency. For no matter how much glory he ascribed to the new covenant administration, the fact was that some didn't perceive it. Paul concedes the point, but hastens to add that the fault lies not with the gospel, but with those who failed to perceive it. Its glory is veiled *to* them because its truth is veiled *in* them.

This power at work within those who are perishing through gospel-rejection is nothing other than 'the god of this age' (verse 4). This is Satan, who darkens the minds, who keeps the light out, so that the Source of light, Jesus Christ, does not shine into their hearts. Throughout this present age Satan exercises a kind of sway, usurping God's place with a power that is temporarily granted by divine permission and limited by divine restrictions. His technique is always to present wrong as right, to teach lies as truth. As the great pretender, Satan masquerades as an angel of light (see 2 Cor. 11:14-15). Tragically, he is far too successful in keeping people from gazing upon 'the light of the gospel of glory in Christ.' (*Question 2*)

The method of ministry in the new covenant is further characterized by the humble content or theme of its preaching. In contrast to false apostles in Corinth, Paul preaches not himself as lord, but Jesus Christ. Paul is but a bondservant, a humble slave to those under his care. His servitude is neither manipulative nor self-serving, but rendered 'for Jesus' sake' (verse 5). Notice that the apostle uses our Savior's personal name here, a name associated with the Lord Jesus Christ in His state of humiliation. This Jesus 'emptied Himself, taking on the form of a bondservant' (Phil. 2:7).

There is no place in the Christian ministry for self-aggrandizement and self-promotion. For salvation is all of God, as verse 6 teaches. Satan's evil action is overcome by God counter-action. Satan spreads darkness; God commands light to shine. Satan sows ignorance; God reveals knowledge. As the Source of light and truth, the God of creation who once brought light into being is also the God of re-creation, who once more commands the light to shine into our hearts at the new birth. To the apostle is given knowledge of God's glory and truth, mediated through the risen, ascended and returning Christ to all who believe on His name.

What a glorious ministry has been given to New Testament apostles and pastors! The *source* of this ministry is God Himself, and its *goal* is found in Jesus Christ, the resplendent image of the invisible God. The surpassing excellence of its power and freedom, its openness and intimacy, is what New Testament ministers are to be busy with each day among God's people. Every minister must himself be illumined by the divine light he seeks to have shine into the hearts and lives of those entrusted to him. A ministry without that experience of glory will necessarily be flat and fruitless, without much joy and benefit to God or men.

Divine glory revealed through ministerial weakness (read 4:7-15)

The little word 'but' introduces in verse 7 the striking contrast between this splendorous glory and its frail, unworthy human vessels. 'We have this treasure,' writes the apostle, 'in earthen vessels, that the excellence of the power may be of God and not of us.' 'Treasure' refers not to the apostle's ministry, but to 'the light of the knowledge of the glory of God in the face of Jesus Christ' (verse 6). The apostle wants to employ the disproportion between the visible means God uses, and their effects, as proof that the gospel's real power lies in God, not in ministers. That is to say: the gospel's content cannot be contained by its servant-vessels, so surpassing is its excellence. This contrast is so great, in order that the gospel's power may be seen to be of God. Such 'divine design' baffles the world, which thinks only in terms of human ability.

How weak are the gospel's messengers? The apostle provides a description of his own ministerial experiences. He speaks of being cornered, but not crushed; being at wits' end, but not at the end of his rope. Paul knew the hostility and hatred of his opponents, suffering beatings at their hands, being thrown out of town and left for dead. But in every instance, there was a limit to his suffering, a boundary to his weakness, so that the power and deliverance of Christ might be shown through him. His was a fellowship in Christ's sufferings (Phil. 3:10), as he identified with his Master's experience and style. But this perpetual dying became the opportunity for Christ's life to be displayed in Paul's mortal body. Death is followed by resurrection. That's how God's power is made perfect in weakness. Such is the pattern of Christ and His apostle, for every believer. The *content* of gospel preaching is eternal life through Christ's atoning death. The *method* of gospel ministry is divine power being magnified through ministerial weakness.

And *living* the gospel life consists of finding oneself by losing and denying oneself! (*Question 3*)

Verse 12 brings home the lesson of apostolic weakness. The Corinthian congregation is the very proof the apostle needs, in order to show that his constant afflictions on behalf of Jesus Christ are not fruitless. These believers are alive, through the Spirit, because he had willingly borne in his body the marks of death. This is the miracle of ministry, that through what is despised and persecuted by the world, God works life eternal.

The attitude of faith is shared with the psalmist who composed Psalm 116. This poem is a song of thanksgiving for deliverance from death. Just as the psalmist's inward faith became manifest in outward speech, so the apostle's experience of 'death,' both by conversion and by persecution, spurred him to testify concerning the victorious, risen Christ. He who raised this Christ Jesus unto glory will raise up all who believe in Him, and present the unblemished bride to her Husband, for an eternity of bliss.

All of these apostolic afflictions are endured, then, for the sake of the Corinthian believers. The goal of endurance is that more people may come to know divine grace through the gospel, so that more gratitude may be expressed, and greater praise offered to God.

Ministerial endurance with an eye to eternal glory (read 4:16-18)

Repeating the exclamation of verse 1, the apostle declares again his ministerial confidence: 'Therefore, we do not lose heart.' In the face of suffering and persecution, outward weakness and decay, as the 'outward man' is constantly dying, yet the 'inward man' is being renewed day by day. What does this mean? By 'outward man' Paul does not mean the 'old man' which the Christian must 'put off' (see Rom. 6:6; Eph. 4:22; Col. 3:9). The reference here is not to our sinful *moral* nature, but to our mortal *physical* nature, our human constitution with all its faculties and energies. By 'inward man' Paul means the inner heart and character of the believer, which is daily renewed by the work of God's Spirit.

What explains this experience-of-contrasts within believers? The inner logic of this experience is explained in verses 17-18 where, by means of comparisons, Paul teaches that affliction is itself part of the process of obtaining surpassing glory. Remember that he's not saying this about any and all human suffering, but only about suffering *for Jesus' sake* (verse 11). This affliction is 'light' only by comparison with the 'heaviness' of divine glory awaiting believers in heaven.

Believers fix their gaze upon invisible realities, not visible ones. To the world, conversion *looks* like loss; discipleship *appears* to be nothing but slavery; piety *seems* like little more than psychological gratification. But the eyes of faith 'see' something different. The Christian sees power in weakness, glory in decay, life in death. All of these are seen first and foremost in the Lord Jesus Christ. He—His suffering, death, resurrection and glorification—is the explanation and the pattern for faith, and for faithful living. (*Question 4*)

These principles that faith sees are eternal, not restricted to a man from Galilee, or to a fellow stopped on a Damascus road. The Corinthian congregation—and all God's people—must make up their minds to accept and glory in such a gospel, brought by such a frail and humble spokesman as Paul. And every faithful minister of the gospel must learn and relearn that God's grace *is*, surprisingly and savingly, made perfect in human weakness. This experiential knowledge sustains him in the face of human opposition, emotional despair, and spiritual suffering in the gospel ministry, to the glory of God and the well-being of the church. (*Questions 5 and 6*)

Questions for Reflection and Reply

1. Every minister has to answer, finally and eternally, to God. How should this comfort and caution both pastor and congregation?

2. What are some tools or strategies that Satan uses to fool people into thinking that what is wrong is right, and what is false is true? How can Satan be successful with his strategies *in the church?* Can the phrase 'those who are perishing' (4:3) refer also to church members? Defend your answer from Scripture.

3. If living the gospel life consists of finding oneself by losing and denying oneself, how does this contradict the false 'gospel' of self-*esteem?* May the pursuit of happiness be the goal of Christian living?

4. What should we mean by 'doing everything to the glory of God'? Why does *losing* something (a basketball game, a job, a loved one) often present a greater opportunity to glorify God than winning?

5. Faith sees that 'loss' is really gain, that human 'weakness' is the occasion for God's power. Mention specific ways that we can apply this to our daily obedience.

6. Mention some specific ways in which you can encourage your minister with the teachings of this lesson.

Lesson 5

2 Corinthians 5:1-11

Gospel Tension Between the Present and the Future

Memory Verse: 'Therefore we are always confident, knowing that while we are at home in the body we are absent from the Lord. For we walk by faith, not by sight. We are confident, yes, well pleased rather to be absent from the body and to be present with the Lord.'

2 Corinthians 5:6-8

Mixed metaphors for the mystery of Christian existence (read 5:1-5)

The Christian life is filled with so many remarkable contrasts. For example, believers value redemption most highly when they consider most deeply the power of sin. Again, although Christians are dead to sin, they still struggle with its power in their lives. And, while they may live on earth, they enjoy traces of heaven in the meantime. These are a few of the tensions that keep faith's bowstring taut.

We heard the apostle compare, in our previous lesson, the 'light' affliction of suffering for Christ's sake with the 'heavy' glory awaiting believers in heaven. (Because our lesson builds so clearly on the preceding verses, please read again 2 Cor. 4:16-18.) Continuing to unfold his theme of gospel power magnified through human weakness, Paul writes with tones of confidence ('we know,' verse 1; 'we are always confident,' verses 6,8) mixed with yearning groans (verses 2,4).

This confidence and these groans describe apostolic experience. Please remember that when Paul employs an array of 'we,' 'us' and 'our' in these verses, he is referring to himself and his missionary companion Timothy. So before we extend these verses to our own experience, we must try to understand them as the apostle's self-description.

Metaphor #1: Earthly tent ⟶ *heavenly house*

Why is Paul confidently persevering in his apostolic work? Because he realizes that in spite of opposition and persecution, indeed, *through* such suffering, he is made to yearn more and more for God to show His power and strength. 'For we know,' he writes, 'that if our earthly house, this tent, is destroyed, we have a building from God, a house not made with hands, eternal in the heavens.'

What is this 'earthly house'? The most likely explanation is that it refers to our earthly mode of existence, in the body. In other words, Paul is saying that if, through suffering and exhausting opposition, his body gives out, his earthly existence ceases, he will receive in its place something better.

Now, let's look carefully at why it will be better.

First, Paul-the-tentmaker observes that this tent of his old existence (denoting impermanence, impoverishment, fragility) will be replaced with a building (stability, durability, beauty). It's a building *from God*, that is: this new mode of existence comes from heaven to earth, not the other way around.

Second, this new dwelling is not manufactured (literally, hand-made), but is spiritual, like the 'circumcision not made with hands' (Col. 2:11) and the 'tabernacle not made with hands' (Heb. 9:11). This new mode of existence is a spiritual creation, not a human invention.

And third, this building from God is 'eternal in the heavens,' relating to Jesus Christ Himself, who has ascended to the Father's right hand as the head of His Body, the church.

Every believer, being in Christ, is therefore a new creation (2 Cor. 5:17), and experiences this tension of a salvation that awaits completion. It can be an exhausting burden, sometimes, to live here on earth. This is what the apostle means in verses 2-4, where he speaks of groaning for and earnestly desiring heaven's way of life, where God's children live in resurrection style. (*Question 1*)

Metaphor #2: New clothes

Notice, then, the mixed metaphor in verses 2-4: Paul writes of being *clothed* with our *dwelling!*

But the metaphor's point becomes plain when we see that he is not speaking of *changing* his clothes, but of being *over-coated*, receiving a new garment to cover his old one. (A more accurate translation, in verse 4, would be: '. . . not because we want to be unclothed, but *further* clothed with our heavenly dwelling . . . .') Normally, people remove their old clothes before putting on the new ones. But Paul wishes to put the second set right over the old clothes. He longs to avoid being unclothed, and would rather be further clothed. How? Through life swallowing up mortality (verse 4).

Here's the point to remember: the principal mystery of Christian living is that 'what is' (mortality) is transformed into 'what shall be' (life eternal). Think of our Lord's post-resurrection body: it was recognizable as His body (continuity) even though it was obviously different (transfiguration)! Similarly, our heavenly existence will display continuity with our earthly existence (we'll have bodies), but with some fundamental changes (we'll have transfigured bodies).

Here we come face to face with the mystery of redemption itself: *continuity through transformation.* This is the mystery of re-generation, for example. Generation we can understand. But *re*-generation? Who ever heard of a seed germinating twice? Or an egg hatching more than once? The very notion of being spiritually 'born *again*' involves being over-coated by the Spirit of God. Imagine yourself looking down on the highway of your own spiritual life. As you compare the 'before' and 'after,' it's clear that what lived before regeneration was truly *you*, and that what lives afterward is the *new you*. (*Question 2*)

Now we begin to sense the holy tension in Christian living, between the present and the future. You see, these two sets of clothing represent two modes of existence. Our existence in the present age is tattered with sin, worn threadbare by the struggle against evil. But along with the apostle, we yearn for the coming age, when God's resurrection power will clothe each of us with a new existence: spotless, wrinkle-free and beautiful. We groan for the coming age when our works will be purified and our bodies healed.

Why do we long so deeply for our new clothes? Because God Himself has created that yearning deep within us, when He gave His Spirit to dwell (again the building metaphor!) within the church. This Holy Spirit is a guarantee—or better: a deposit—of the coming new age. Quite unlike the guarantees we receive with our home appliances, this deposit is of the same nature as the thing guaranteed, a first install-ment. This means that there can be no failure or frustration of God's plan for believers! His own Spirit serves as an internal life-force, working powerfully within, assuring all believers that the very same power at work in Christ's resurrection and in their regeneration is preparing their mortal bodies for the consummation of redemption. *Having experienced re-generation, we now long for the completion of God's re-creation!* (*Question 3*)

Application #1: Confidence for the present (read 5:6-8)

The apostle turns now to apply his metaphors of Christian existence to his own apostolic life and labors. He speaks of a constant, present-day confidence ('always confident'), a certainty not dependent on moods or circumstances. His courage is enhanced by knowledge: 'knowing that while we are at home in the body we are absent from the Lord.'

Scripture does not mean to suggest here that anyone who feels 'at home' in this life is thereby not living close to Christ. Nor are we to learn from this passage that Christ is not near to those on earth who love and believe in Him. Rather, the phrases 'at home' and 'absent' describe two kinds of existence, consistent with the thought of the preceding verses.

Another description is found in verse 7: 'For we walk by faith, not by sight.' Throughout the Bible, the metaphor of 'walking' describes *living*, following the path either of obedience or of sin (see Psalm 1, for example). Believers living after Pentecost 'walk' not according to the flesh, but by the Spirit (Rom. 8:1). Here in verse 7, two quite distinct manners of living are identified: 'by faith' and 'by sight.' These describe different orientations, distinct mind-sets, contrasting life-principles.

But let us be careful to understand *from the context* how 'faith' and 'sight' are related. Remember what we learned earlier: the main point of the clothing metaphor was *continuity through transformation* (mortality is swallowed up by life). Similarly, 'faith' is the overcoat covering 'sight.' Faith goes deeper, reaches higher, encompasses more, than sight. *The problem is not that 'sight' is always wrong, but that it's never enough! It is by faith—not as instrument, but as necessary condition—that God transforms mere sight into perspective.* As the apostle had put it a few verses earlier: 'the things which are seen are temporary, but the things which are not seen are eternal' (2 Cor. 4:18).

One reason for pausing to reflect on the relationship between these two manners of existence is the common assertion that faith *contradicts* sight. But this way of putting the matter seems to confuse the categories of faith/sight with those of flesh/Spirit. Without question, the Spirit contradicts and opposes the flesh (see Gal. 5:16ff., where 'flesh' denotes the old way of life-governed-by-sin). But not so with 'faith' and 'sight.' The problem with living by sight is not inaccuracy, but inadequacy. As Hebrews 11:1 teaches: 'Now faith is the substance of things hoped for, the evidence of things not seen.' (*Question 4*)

Summarizing the apostle's point, then, we learn that although the believer's future manner of life will be better than his present earthly existence, the certain coming of heavenly glory encourages us to prepare now, by the way we live, to enjoy our 'new clothes.'

Application #2: Confidence for the future (read 5:9-11)

If our deepest desire is to be transformed, finally, into the image of

Christ, then that longing must fuel our daily progress toward Christlikeness. Another motive for present faithfulness is the future judgment. We desire to please God with an eye to standing, one day, before His throne of judgment, where everything done on earth will undergo scrutiny and evaluation.

Therein lies the meaning of the final judgment for the believer: it is a judgment of *evaluation*, not *condemnation*. Divine rewards, proceeding from grace, varying in proportion according to our earthly performance, await us in heaven. (*Question 5*)

Knowing the terror of the Lord (verse 11; notice, again, how much the Christian faith involves *knowing!*), the apostle is filled with reverential awe for his Master and solemn regard for his own ministry. This realization compels him to persuade those within the Corinthian congregation who doubt his sincerity and challenge his apostolic authority. Deep down, they know he's right. In their consciences (that private 'throne of judgment,' where the absolute demands of a holy God are privately applied), they know that Paul is whole-hearted and single-minded in his presentation of the claims of Christ. Consequently, in view of both the coming eternal judgment before God, and the present temporal judgment among the Corinthians, the apostle acknowledges his own integrity and willingness to be well-pleasing to God.

Questions for Reflection and Reply

1. Mention some traces of heaven that believer enjoy on earth already now.

2. Compare the meanings of the word 'new' in the following statements: 'Last week I bought a new car' and 'When that carpenter was finished remodeling, I had a new kitchen!' Which statement depicts 'continuity through transformation'? In which of these two senses will we have 'new' bodies in heaven?

3. Mention some ways in which a believer's longing 'for the completion of God's re-creation' comes to expression. What are some benefits and dangers of singing songs that focus on 'getting to heaven'?

4. The believer knows that 'sight' is never enough; by faith God transforms mere *sight* into *perspective*. Illustrate this with regard to suffering persecution, a loss of any kind, and world events.

5. In light of *Heidelberg Catechism*, Lord's Day 19, QA 52, why should we look forward to the last judgment? Why don't we, so often?

Lesson 6

2 Corinthians 5:12-21

The Ministry of Divine Reconciliation

Memory Verse: '. . . and [Christ] died for all, that those who live should
no longer live for themselves, but for Him who died for
them and rose again.'

2 Corinthians 5:15

Apostolic antidote for a poisoned congregation (read 5:12-13)

You will recall from Lesson 1 that one of the main purposes of this
epistle is apostolic self-defense to a congregation being poisoned by
notions advanced by false teachers. In Paul's day, even as in our own,
God's people were being infected by competing views of the ministry,
by rival opinions concerning the nature of Christian living and of the
church. Paul's critics were accusing him of insincerity, religious extrem-
ism, and self-promotion (see 2 Cor. 10:7-11; 11:5-15). In order to
administer the proper antidote, the apostle in turn was identifying his
opponents as those who relied on externals—on appearance, on showi-
ness, on clever techniques and tactics (see 2 Cor. 4:2; 5:12).

In the preceding chapters, then, Paul has been offering the Corinthian believers the serum with which to counteract the venom of these
false teachers. He's been saying, as it were: 'Do you want something to
brag about? Brag about this: our ministry toward you proceeds from
the fear of God, not the fear of men.' Here in verses 12-13, he coun-
ters by saying, 'To those who complain that I'm a religious maniac, tell
them that my imbalance is for your sakes; let God handle my fanati-
cism—you simply listen to my sober-minded appeal that you be reconciled to the Lord. My sincerity is evident in my motive and message:
that you be reconciled to God in Christ Jesus.' *(Question 1)*

The compelling motive for the Christian ministry (read 5:14-15)

With these verses, we enter one of the most sublime portions of sacred Scripture. Be aware that there is, in the remaining verses of this chapter, far too much material to exhaust in this Bible study lesson. But let's not permit the glorious splendor to frighten us away from drawing near to gaze on the beauty of God's redemption.

Since his conversion, the great compelling motive in the apostle's life was *love*, a love which began with God and returned to Him. It was the love of Christ for Paul, more than Paul's love for Christ, that drove him to proclaim as his fixed conviction that God's redemption was accomplished by Christ's *substitutionary* death. Divine love is unavailable, and unintelligible, apart from *this kind* of death.

There are other kinds of death: the heroic death of a soldier, the exemplary death of a martyr, the penal death of a criminal. Christ's was none of these. His was the death of a righteous Man for the unrighteous.

Notice the connection being pressed by Paul: 'If One died for all, then all died.' Both verbs point back to the same event, namely, Christ's crucifixion. The same apostle teaches in Romans 5:12-21 similarly that when the *one* man Adam sinned, death (sin's penalty) passed on to *all* men, since all had sinned. Even so, all those who belong to Christ are, through the power of His resurrection, made alive unto God. 'He died for all, that those who live should live no longer for themselves, but for Him who died for them and rose again' (2 Cor. 5:15). (*Question 2*)

Just as the apostle no longer lived for himself, willingly placing even his flesh in service to the gospel, so the Corinthian believers—and all who are made alive by Christ's Spirit—must no longer live for themselves, but for Christ Jesus, their once-dead, now risen Savior.

Two radical dimensions of living for Christ (read 5:16-17)

Living for Christ Jesus entails a radically new assessment of others, including of our Savior (verse 16), and of ourselves (verse 17).

The apostle acknowledges that 'from now on' (the time of his conversion), his appraisal of others is no longer 'according to the flesh.' He no longer evaluates people by the world's standards of value, standards measuring only outward dimensions like race, social status, wealth and power.

The clearest and most straightforward explanation of verse 16b ('Even though we have known Christ according to the flesh, yet now we know Him thus no longer.') is that prior to his conversion, Paul's knowledge of Christ had been according to human standards (think of his persecution of early Christians—of Christ Himself, really); but with his conversion came the transformation of his knowledge of Christ. He now knew Christ 'for real.'

And how must we view *ourselves*, then? Anyone who has died and risen with Christ is, in fact, a new creation. With those two words, *'in Christ*,' the apostle summarizes the inexhaustible significance of divine redemption. Being 'in' Christ means taking refuge in God's acceptable surety; it speaks of a future inheritance with Him who reigns over all things. To be 'in' Christ is to enjoy access to Truth, and power for doing Right. As Philip Hughes writes in his commentary on this verse, all these descriptions of redemption attempt to capture this glorious reality, that 'redemption in Christ is nothing less than the fulfillment of God's eternal purposes in creation.'

This view of ourselves extends, really, to all of creation: 'old things have passed away; behold, all things have become new.' Notice first the past tense, pointing to the time of regeneration and conversion, when all those fleshly enslavements and prejudices became, suddenly, 'old.' At that distinct point in time, they could be described as 'former,' as 'past.' In their place arose newness of life, a newness that is and continues forever new, never fading.

Observe also that while there is a definite *discontinuity* between old and new (old things *have passed away*), there is at the same time a certain *continuity* (all things *have become* new). In our previous lesson we saw this truth applied in terms of the earthly and heavenly modes of existence. Here, Scripture expands the principle to a cosmic scale: *all things* have become new. What a glory-filled comfort for the believer! The heart-experience of a child of God, born anew and raised to life 'in Christ,' is part and parcel of the future cosmic re-new-al, including the new heavens and the new earth!

The essential character of the Christian ministry (read 5:18-21)

Whenever Scripture speaks of creation, it speaks of God as the originating source. So too in redemption. It was this God who, while His children lived in rebellious enmity toward Him, sent His Son as Mediator and atonement for sin. Redemption's plan and its execution depend solely on God.

The heart of redemption is reconciliation, which in turn presupposes alienation. The cause of alienation is sin. By his sin, man has both offended God and brought God's wrath down upon himself. Together, *human offense* and *divine wrath* are the components of alienation. The only possible way to replace alienation with reconciliation is for God to provide another Suitable Object who has not offended His holiness and upon whom He may pour out His wrath.

So God matched—rather: overpowered—man's rebellion by His love, sending His Son. But never forget that the purpose of divine love includes—and does not contradict—the satisfaction of divine wrath for human sin. The cross of Jesus Christ is the emblem of God's love only *because* it is the altar of His anger. There, at the cross, mercy combined with truth, and justice embraced peace (Ps. 85:10).

Having opened the *way* of reconciliation through the blood of Christ, God has entrusted to His servants the *ministry* of reconciliation.

What kind of ministry is this? Preeminently, it is a ministry of proclamation. God has committed to (literally: deposited in) His servants 'the *word* of reconciliation,' a deposit that has transformed these messengers, and requisitioned them as heralds of the very grace that has renewed them.

The content of their message is profoundly simple: 'God was in Christ reconciling the world to Himself, not imputing their trespasses to them.' The *source* reconciliation is *God-in-Christ*. The *scope* of reconciliation is *the world*. And the *basis* of reconciliation is *acquittal*.

On the one hand, this divine reconciliation was accomplished once for all, at the cross. But, as verse 20 indicates, this reconciliation is applied and therefore becomes personally real to believers through the ministry of God's own ambassadors. An ambassador acts and speaks on behalf of *and* in the place of the sovereign. Notice that the apostle doesn't say, 'Therefore we are *like* ambassadors for Christ,' but quite simply, 'we *are* ambassadors for Christ.' God makes His plea (what a gracious Sovereign, that He should plead with us—the offenders!—to be reconciled with Him!) through His ministers.

Faithful to their commission, gospel ministers *implore* their hearers to be reconciled to God. On behalf of their Savior and Sender, they beseech and plead, they persuade and coax.

Why should their hearers respond? Because God made Christ Jesus, who was without sin, to *be sin* on behalf of those who had forfeited divine favor and fellowship. This is the ground and basis upon which reconciliation has been extended, and an essential ingredient to the summons of preaching. The sinlessness of Christ is absolutely necessary for restored fellowship, for only He was able to bear the sin of others.

Scripture tells us here that God made Christ Jesus not a *sinner*, but *sin*. That is: God made His Son the object of His wrath and judgment, pouring upon Him the punishment sin deserved, in order to remove the sin of the world. The logic of reconciliation stipulates that *forgiveness follows satisfaction* (satisfactory payment). Reconciliation requires both propitiation (appeasing divine wrath) and expiation (providing a covering for sin). (*Question 3*)

41

If Christ was made to *be sin*, the apostle declares that believers have become, not righteous, but *righteousness*—even more: they have become the righteousness *of God*. This refers to the believer's justification, whereby his sins are credited to Christ, and the Savior's spotless perfection is reckoned to the believer's account. Here it is useful to distinguish between the instantaneous righteousness afforded in justification, and the progressively growing personal righteousness of sanctification. The first is the source of the second, and they both find their fullness at glorification.

All of this speaks of power, divine power in the face of human weakness and sin. Every minister of the gospel, and everyone ministered to by the gospel, knows that this God-wrought reconciliation is what distinguishes Christianity from every other religion. 'God was in Christ reconciling the world to Himself, not imputing their trespasses to them.' That is the heart of the gospel, the church's *raison d'etre* or reason for existence. And as the apostle himself knew so well, this is the heart of the gospel *ministry* and its *only* justification! (*Questions 4 and 5*)

Questions for Reflection and Reply

1. Why is it difficult for a person to prove his sincerity? How should we determine whether or not a minister is sincere? Should we even be concerned about that? Why (not)?

2. Read either the *Canons of Dort*, Second Head, Articles 3 and 8, and accompanying Rejection of Errors, Paragraph 5; or *The Westminster Confession of Faith*, Chapter VIII, Paragraphs v.-viii. Explain what it means that Christ's death was *sufficient* for all people, but *efficient* only for the elect. Why is this distinction necessary? What is the doctrine of universalism? Why does universalism eventually result in an empty church?

3. If there can be no forgiveness without satisfactory payment, neither can there be forgiveness without repentance. Both recognize the presence of guilt. What results in the church when forgiveness is offered—even promised—where there is no repentance? Identify healthy and unhealthy ways in which preaching can emphasize guilt.

4. May a Christian work for social, political and economic 'reconciliation' in the world without *first* seeking spiritual reconciliation? Why (not)? Can reconciliation with God occur without reconciliation with man? Explain how the two are related.

5. What kind of 'solutions' do non-Christian religions offer to the problems of alienation and suffering? Think of Hinduism, Buddhism, Islam, etc.

Lesson 7

2 Corinthians 6:1-7:1

Ministerial Hardship for the sake of Gospel Holiness

Memory Verse: 'Therefore, having these promises, beloved, let us cleanse ourselves from all filthiness of the flesh and spirit, perfecting holiness in the fear of God.'

2 Corinthians 7:1

An urgent and blameless ministry (read 6:1-3)

So exalted is the ministry of reconciliation that the apostle describes it as 'working together' with God (NKJV). This co-operation is evident from the fact that not only does *God* plead with the Corinthians (2 Cor. 5:20), but now Paul and Timothy plead with them too.

The content of their plea is that this congregation not receive God's grace in vain. What does it mean to receive God's grace *in vain?* Does this refer to what Christ meant in His parable of the four soils, when He described those who receive the gospel with joy but, having no root, fall away and wither in times of affliction? Or could the apostle be expressing here the possibility that someone who has received grace can lose it?

It's not likely that the apostle is thinking here of superficial faith or final perseverance. Rather, he writes with the awareness that false apostles had come into the congregation, peddling a different gospel, different from what they had received before. Receiving God's grace in vain, then, meant living inconsistently with their profession, denying the implications of the gospel, one of which was that Christ died so that they might live no longer to themselves, but to His glory (2 Cor. 5:15).

The quote, in verse 2, from Isaiah 49:8 reminds Paul's readers of those glorious days of repentance and conversion, when under Paul's ministry they had received the gift of salvation. His powerful proclamation, weak though Paul himself may have been, was the dawn of the day of salvation. The 'time' of grace and repentance is acceptable *to God*, since He appointed its beginning and end. This places man in a position of favor and opportunity, but also one of responsibility: he needs to answer the divine summons!

Now, sometimes urgency provides the excuse to cut corners or employ questionable means. But not for Paul, who insists, 'we give no offense in anything, that our ministry may not be blamed' (verse 3). Not only Christians, but especially ministers and other church leaders must walk consistently with their profession. Any fleck of hypocrisy and contradiction will smirch the name of Christ and the gospel of His grace. As Philip Hughes remarks, 'The preaching of the cross, it is true, inevitably gives offence to the unregenerate mind which is governed by pride and self-esteem (cf. 1 Cor. 1:23; Gal. 5:11); but for the messenger of reconciliation to place a stumblingblock in the way of unbelievers by behaviour which is improper and inconsistent with his message is quite another thing, and altogether inexcusable.' (*Question 1*)

Ministerial hardships as occasions for endurance (read 6:4-10)

It isn't easy being a minister of reconciliation. If you read these verses 4-10, you likely wondered how any man alive could put up with such a variety of troubles! But put up with them Paul did, with much patience and endurance. One attempt to arrange the trials mentioned in verses 4-5 organizes them this way:

- *General trials:* tribulations, needs, distresses
- *Specific persecutions:* beatings, imprisonments, riots
- *Voluntary deprivations:* labors, sleepless nights, fasts

The apostle begins with the most general afflictions that a minister is called to endure. His vows and duties may very well bring him into situations of testing and into unavoidable circumstances. At times he will be utterly perplexed by apparently insoluble problems. These, again, are nothing but opportunities for Christ's power to be magnified through human weakness!

Anyone familiar with Paul's personal history, through the book of Acts or his epistles, can identify incidents where he was beaten, imprisoned or became the center of a riot. Riots, for example, occurred on account of Paul and his message in Pisidian Antioch, Iconium, Lystra, Philippi, Corinth, Ephesus and Jerusalem.

Voluntary hardships included hard work, nights without sleep, and hunger. So consumed was he by his calling and ministry, that Paul sacrificed those things many consider necessities of life.

After describing the variety of trials that come to a minister of the gospel, the apostle next sets forth, in verses 6-10, the spiritual qualities and means by which endurance is possible. These include *purity* of life and motive; *knowledge* of the truth in Christ Jesus; *forbearance* with those in the churches who reviled him; *kindness*; the *Holy Spirit* who here 'is nearly equivalent to the spirit of holiness which ought to be the central feature of the ministerial character'; and *unfeigned love*, the primary fruit of the Spirit.

The very message he proclaimed testified to Paul's sincerity and blamelessness, which was accompanied by divine power sufficient to change the life of his Corinthian readers. Picking up a military metaphor, the apostle ascribes his endurance to 'the armor of righteousness on the right hand and on the left,' that is: weapons that can withstand the test of righteousness and that serve the cause of justice, preparing the soldier to meet attack from any quarter, equipped with offensive weapons (right hand) as well as defensive (left hand).

Verse 8 begins a series of contrasts worth pondering. The first is between honor and dishonor, and suggests that the minister of Christ is usually the subject of flimsy and fickle opinions. He has close friends and bitter foes; the former respect him, the latter insult and revile him. If the first contrast pictures the personal treatment of the apostle, the second comparison describes what went on behind his back: 'by evil report and good report.' In both situations, Paul demonstrated patient endurance and pastoral integrity, resisting the impulses of vengeance and pride.

One of the evil reports about Paul that had been circulating was that he was a deceiver, an imposter. Yet he argues from a clear conscience that he maintained sincerity of motive and integrity of character. As one enlisted into Christ's mission separately on the Damascus road, he was not recognized as a credentialed apostle. Nor did he enjoy widespread fame among the world. And yet, as any lamb in Christ's flock, he was well-known by his God and Savior. Although many of his troubles brought him to the brink of death, the resurrection gospel of Christ sustained him, and from his position in Christ he continually experienced the power of eternal life. And though his enemies pronounced his sufferings to be the mark of divine wrath and punishment, the apostle bore witness that the Lord's purpose was not to kill, but to bless.

Every serious minister suffers the sorrow caused by fair-weather friends, the heartache of rejection by backslidden converts, the pain of serving carnal church members. Tears fall because the gospel is rejected, families are torn apart, sickness and death invade the congregation. Yet, through all of his sorrows, the apostle rejoiced, heeding his own counsel to Philippian believers: 'Rejoice in the Lord always. Again I will say, rejoice!' (Phil. 4:4). Even Paul's poverty, visible to all, became the occasion for enriching others, as the Savior crowned his preaching with changing lives.

Indeed, with a climax so contradictory to the eye of flesh, the apostle ends his litany: 'as having nothing, and yet possessing all things.' Why was this pauper really a king? Because, as he had told the Corinthians earlier (1 Cor. 3:21ff.), he was Christ's, and Christ was his!

With this, Paul has finished speaking of his ministerial integrity, not to exalt himself, but to exalt the glory-filled gospel of reconciliation, whose ambassador he was. Each of his apostolic trials, and all of them together, provided occasion for God to magnify His power and grace, both in the life of His servant *and in the eyes of His people! (Questions 2, 3 and 4)*

Ministerial love longing to be requited (read 6:11-13)

Time and again the apostle has opened his heart to these believers, commending himself to their consciences, inviting their scrutiny. Now with a spontaneous outburst of tender urging, he asks them to pay him the same kindness: to welcome him and to listen to his defense with hearts as wide as his own. In spite of the hardships they had caused their missionary-pastor, Paul's affection wasn't limited in the least. Nor was his love a restricting, cloying attachment, designed to manipulate the congregation into following him; the apostle was no cult leader! If there was any restriction, it was in their affections, which were diluted by a spirit of meanness and suspicion generated by enemies and religious imposters.

Like a parent coaxing a child, with enticements like 'Now say thank you' and 'Go ahead, you shake his hand too,' the apostle invites the Corinthian congregation to 'love him back.' Relying on more than mere logic and evidence, this pastor appeals to something words can hardly express: to a bond and a mutual identity no pretender could fake.

A call to congregational holiness (read 6:14-7:1)

Here for the first time in this letter we read specific moral instruction from the apostle's pen. The principle he wants to drive home is expressed first by a metaphor of a double yoke under which two animals work side by side. This very metaphor had earlier been an Old Testament stipulation for farming: 'You shall not plow with an ox and a donkey together' (Deut. 22:10). Next, in verses 14b-16a the apostle asks a series of rhetorical questions whose answer should be obvious:

Question: What fellowship has righteousness with lawlessness?
Answer: None. They're opposites.

Question: What communion has light with darkness?
Answer: None. They've been separated since creation!

Question: What accord has Christ with Belial?
Answer: None. They're mortal enemies!

Then Paul puts his point in the form of a question:

Question: What part has a believer with an unbeliever?
Answer: None, really.

Question: What agreement has the temple of God with idols?
Answer: None, because *God* won't plow with anybody else!

Underlying each of these questions is the formula '*x* is incompatible with *y*.' (*Question 5*)

Now follows something very profound. Without stopping to explain himself, Paul immediately adds in verse 16: 'For *you* are *the* temple of the living God.' The 'you' (or 'we') is *plural*, the comparison is *singular*. True enough, Paul emphasizes elsewhere that *each believer* is a temple of the Holy Spirit (see 1 Cor. 6:19f.). But his point here is that *the entire congregation* is the temple of the living God. Combining the sense of Leviticus 26:12, Jeremiah 32:28 and Ezekiel 37:27, the apostle argues in effect that the New Testament congregation is the fulfillment of the Old Testament promise that God would make His dwelling among men, not merely through the incarnation, but (during the time between Pentecost and the second coming) *in the church*.

This profound realization serves as the bridge between Paul's negative exhortation ('be not unequally yoked') and his positive instruction: 'come out from among them.' Again he combines a number of Old Testament allusions (Isa. 52:11; Ezek. 20:34,41) spoken originally as a warning about impending captivity on account of religious compromise, repeated now in order to urge these believers to avoid a similar spiritual destiny by virtue of their compromises with uncleanness. The promise for those who keep themselves unsoiled and unspotted with the world is that God will *receive* them. Being received by God is exactly the 'fellowship,' 'communion,' 'accord' and 'participation' between believers and unbelievers prohibited earlier in verses 14-16a.

The quality of this reception is indicated by verse 18: 'I will be a

Father to you, and you shall be My sons and daughters, says the LORD Almighty.' These words hark back to 2 Samuel 7:8, 14, to a message spoken originally to David about his son who would succeed him as king. So, then, there are three 'stages' in which this Old Testament prophecy was fulfilled, represented in sequence by Solomon, Jesus Christ, and all those who by faith are engrafted into Christ. God has received us into His fellowship, welcoming us with an open heart as our tender Father for Christ's sake.

To these 'beloved' who possess such rich promises of fellowship and participation in Christ, comes the exhortation to make a complete break with every form of compromise, both external and internal. That is what believers are to flee *from*.

What they are to flee *after* is 'perfecting holiness in the fear of God.' This pursuit is both continual and reverential. Holiness is not something that comes all at once; it is a process of development in the Christian life, growing in Christ-likeness, called sanctification. But its source and strength is God. Our holiness is *from* God and *to* God, *through* Him and *in* Him.

Fleeing *after* holiness can never occur without fleeing *from* sin. They proceed simultaneously, as a single motion. The energy fueling this 'holy motion' is the promise that the LORD is in His holy temple (dwelling among the congregation), and that His holiness obligates us to continual repentance from sin and separation from evil. This is the condition—not meritorious, of course, but necessary circumstance—for being received and sustained in divine fellowship, as children of the Heavenly Father. (*Question 6*)

Questions for Reflection and Reply

1. Mention several ways in which some ministers today give offense, and bring disrepute upon their ministry. May we expect more in the way of spirituality and integrity from ministers than from other church members? Why (not)?

2. Do gospel ministers in North America suffer very much today? Mention several examples of possible *private* suffering that a minister may need to endure. When you think about Paul's life and labors, what are some possible benefits of *public* ministerial hardship?

3. Should the *congregation* be given periodic opportunities to evaluate the pastor's performance? Why (not)? Isn't this strictly the responsibility of the *elders?*

4. What are some effects of paying the minister too much? Too little? Why should(n't) ministers be required to have outside jobs, in addition to church work?

5. The formula '*x* is incompatible with *y*' describes what is called 'the *antithesis.*' God created and sustains every moral and spiritual incompatibility, and Satan wants to erase them. One of his tricks is to paint a pair of incompatibles (honesty / dishonesty) to look like two sides of the same coin (male/female)—not really *opposites*, just *different* from each other.
Let's test our feel for the antithesis. Behind each statement, write 'yes,' 'no' or 'maybe,' and why.

   ● 'Christian *education* and state-sponsored education are incompatible.'

   ● 'Christian *schools* and state-sponsored schools are incompatible.'

   ● 'Christian *students* and non-Christian students are incompatible.'

6. If fleeing *from* iniquity and fleeing *after* holiness occur simultaneously, then *both* provide the biblical basis for Christian schools. In that light, can Christian schools (including colleges!) survive if they are dependent on public (i.e., government) funding, use secular textbooks, and heed the direction of humanistic policy-makers? If not, how can they survive?

Lesson 8

2 Corinthians 7:2-16

Pastoral Joy over the Fruits of Godly Sorrow

Memory Verse: 'For godly sorrow produces repentance to salvation, not to be regretted; but the sorrow of the world produces death.'

2 Corinthians 7:10

Prelude to pastoral praise (read 7:1-4)

Resuming his appeal begun in chapter 6:11-13 ('we have spoken openly to you, our heart is wide open'), the apostle pleads that the Corinthian believers respond in kind by making room for him in their heart. Either in reply to charges being made against him, or in contrast to the practices of false apostles, Paul claims that his ministry has been free of wrongdoing, of corrupt results, and of personal gain through financial fraud.

Before anyone can point to his pleading as an implicit criticism of these believers, the apostle adds that his request is *not* an accusation. In fact, so deep is his love for them that he says, 'You are in our hearts, to die together and to live together.' Pastoral love deeper than this doesn't exist! It withstands even death, and the turmoil of new believers growing in the grace of obedience to the gospel.

How many pastors speak like this to their congregations?

Paul did, and with boasting, according to verse 4: 'Great is my boldness of speech toward you, great is my boasting on your behalf.' His boldness of speech arises from a heart-confidence that they have 'come around' to follow Christ more faithfully. As we shall see in the following verses, Paul's pride in their penitent change is not self-congratulation, but gratitude to God for *His* transforming grace. There is a place in the Christian ministry (even as there is in the Christian life!) for glorying, for boasting, and for pride—so long as it remains *selfless* glorying *in the Lord* (see 2 Cor. 10:17). (*Question 1*)

Their spiritual change occasions more than boasting. It provides this pastor-apostle with deep comfort and abounding joy in the midst of his present afflictions. He had heard the report of Titus (see verse 7), whose thrilling and positive testimony he now proceeds to recount, for the encouragement of the congregation in Corinth. (Here's an example of *good* 'gossip'!)

Consoled by the report of a co-laborer (read 7:5-7)

Paul resumes the discussion he left at 2 Corinthians 2:13. We may view the intervening material (2:14-7:4) as a parenthesis, and understand that the apostle now returns to the theme of awaiting Titus' report concerning the Corinthian situation. In 2:12-13 we learned that after dispatching Titus to Corinth, Paul had gone to Troas, where he had expected to find Titus and hear his news. Unable to wait there for him any longer, the apostle had moved on to Macedonia, where he worked among the churches. Once there, his troubling anxiety didn't disappear, but completely enveloped him: 'outside were conflicts, inside were fears' (7:5b).

Yet, in faithfulness to the prophetic word spoken through Isaiah (49:13), the Lord comforted the apostle through the arrival of his fellow pastor, Titus, who brought the longed-awaited news about the Corinthians and about the effect of Paul's earlier letter.

Not only Paul, but Titus himself had been encouraged by what he heard and saw in the church. In contrast to the anxiety and misgivings of Paul, the congregation displayed ardent longing for the apostle, along with sincere sorrow for all the grief they had given him. This longing and sorrow had given birth to renewed zeal and enthusiasm for spiritual things, further evidence of their transformation.

'Like a father to his children . . .' (read 7:8-12)

In these verses Paul provides a tender explanation of his pastoral emotions and motives behind his prior letter. He realized, perhaps already as he was writing 1 Corinthians, and surely from Titus' report, that his letter would bring them to tears. He didn't regret their sorrow, but he had cringed from the pain of having to discipline them spiritually. Like a father is grieved when he finds it necessary to punish his child, but yet delights in the result brought about by that discipline, the apostle exposes his pastoral heart-motives in this second letter.

Regret is followed by rejoicing. Paul is happy, not about their tears, but about the fruit of their tears, namely: repentance and a change of life. Theirs was a *godly* sorrow, the kind that accompanies repentance which leads to salvation. Nobody ever needs to be ashamed of those tears or that kind of sorrow. Neither those who experience that sorrow, nor pastor-preachers whose labor and instruction occasion such sorrow, should ever regret tears of repentance. While repentance is not the ground or basis of salvation, it is the sign of God's grace busy at work. Without repentance we cannot be saved. (*Questions 2, 3 and 4*)

But there is another kind of sorrow, called here 'the sorrow of the world.' Its fruit is not repentance-unto-salvation, but *death*. This sorrow grieves, to be sure, but only about the painful consequences of sin, not about the sin itself. This kind of sorrow centers upon *self*, and has much in common with self-pity. Compare, for examples of this sorrow in the face of sin, the lives of Esau (read Heb. 12:16f.) and David (read Ps. 51:2ff.). Esau's grief grew into bitter rejection of the covenant, whereas David's sorrow was changed by divine grace into godly joy (Ps. 51:12ff.).

The Corinthians furnished further evidence of repentance, indicated in verse 11. Titus reported that their godly sorrow had produced

- new spiritual diligence;
- an eagerness to clear themselves (in contrast to their former apathy and indifference);
- indignation with themselves for permitting this scandal to go on so long in the church;
- a fear of Paul, that he might come to them with words of divine judgment (see 1 Cor. 4:21);
- a sincere longing to see their relationship with the apostle restored;
- a renewed zeal for the truth, for honoring the apostle's authority among the congregation; and
- a readiness to discipline the wrongdoer, as Paul had instructed them.

Paul speaks here like a father, deeply gratified and humbled that his discipline had such a profound effect. (*Question 5*)

What an important pastoral lesson the Holy Spirit teaches us here! As verse 12 indicates, Paul's primary goal in writing 1 Corinthians had not been to 'get' the wrongdoer, or even to 'save' the victim, but to rescue *the congregation* from certain destruction under God's wrath if they failed to exercise discipline. It wasn't that he was disinterested in the offender, or indifferent to the victim, but by comparison the spiritual repentance of the congregation weighed much more heavily on his heart. His affection *for them* had given birth to the heavy rebuke that in turn had born the fruit of heartfelt congregational conversion. That's what he wanted them to see.

Joy multiplied as compliments are confirmed (read 7:13-16)

Paul returns to what he had been saying in verse 6 about the comfort derived from Titus' arrival. Paul's joy came not only from Titus' *report*, but also from his co-worker's *response* to what he had seen and heard. Titus had been refreshed in spirit by his visit with the congregation, and had related his news with obvious enthusiastic thanksgiving. This in turn had encouraged Paul.

When he had spoken earlier to Titus about the Corinthians' receiving the gospel and God's grace, he had assured him that in spite of their ecclesiastical weaknesses and sins, they had still kept their basic commitment to the gospel. Paul had sent Titus to Corinth with this pastoral endorsement, and events had not disproved him. Paul's word was reliable—not only his word of preaching, but his word of pastoral evaluation as well!

What a supreme example we have here of Christian pastoral care. Paul never hesitated to reprimand, but neither did he shrink from complimenting and encouraging believers. Loving encouragement is as important and necessary a means of discipline as righteous rebuke. His evaluation of the congregation and its problems was balanced, realistic, and fair. Though Titus may have left for Corinth with apprehensions, his attitude had not been poisoned by Paul with any pastoral cynicism. He could return speaking of his affection for these believers, whom he now fondly remembered as obedient to the apostolic message. (*Question 6*)

Such obedience is the mark of a prosperous church. We might well pause here, in view of much contemporary talk about the 'growing church' instead of the 'true church,' to inquire about what makes the church of Jesus Christ prosper, and what makes for an effective and joyful ministry. Notice that in verse 15 the apostle observes that the church received Titus 'with fear and trembling.' These words describe, says Calvin,

> 'what is a right reception for the ministers of Christ. Assuredly, it is not sumptuous banquets, it is not splendid apparel, it is not courteous and honourable salutations, it is not the plaudits of the multitude, that gratify the upright and faithful pastor. He experiences, on the other hand, an overflowing of delight, when the doctrine of salvation is received with reverence from his mouth, when he retains the authority that belongs to him for the edification

of the Church, when the people give themselves up to his direction, to be regulated by his ministry under Christ's banners.' (*Question 7*)

The Corinthians' affectionate reception of Titus emboldened the apostle to greater confidence. He is prepared now to move on to another matter, to his appeal for financial assistance for impoverished co-believers in Jerusalem. The church's conduct, and Titus' joyful report, have given him the signal he needs to urge them on toward still greater unity and faithfulness.

Questions for Reflection and Reply

1. Do you agree that there is a place in the Christian life for boasting? Why is this dangerous for believers to do? Try to write a careful, biblical definition or description of *Christian* boasting.

2. After you consult either the *Heidelberg Catechism* (Lord's Day 33, QA 89) or the *Westminster Larger Catechism* (QA 76), define 'repentance.'

3. How can we teach children to have godly sorrow instead of worldly sorrow?

4. Sometimes people say that preachers should emphasize the 'joy of salvation' more than the 'awareness of sin.' Explain why this is a bad choice, or a false dilemma.

5. Read once again that list of the fruits of godly sorrow. Comment on this claim: *A congregation that does not display these fruits is not living penitently before God.* Explain why you agree or disagree. Why is it a minister's joy to preach and minister God's Word to a *penitent* congregation?

6. How can you help your minister evaluate problems in the church fairly? Why do people so often view church problems in terms of *personality* rather than principle? Should a minister mention congregational problems from the pulpit? Why (not)? Find biblical evidence to support your answer.

7. Read Calvin's advice once more. What specific behavior on the part of church members shows reverence for the minister's teaching and spiritual leadership?

Lesson 9

2 Corinthians 8:1-24

Ministerial Encouragement for the Communion of the Saints (1)

Memory Verse: 'For you know the grace of our Lord Jesus Christ, that though He was rich, yet for your sakes He became poor, that you through His poverty might become rich.'

2 Corinthians 8:9

The communion of saints as divine grace (read 8:1-7)

'What do you understand by *the communion of saints?*' asks the *Heidelberg Catechism.* 'First, that believers, all and every one, as members of Christ, are partakers of Him and of all His treasures and gifts; second, that every one must know himself bound to employ his gifts readily and cheerfully for the advantage and salvation of other members' (QA 55).

That is exactly what we'll be considering in this lesson and the next, as we study 2 Corinthians 8:1-9:15. This extensive passage contains the apostle Paul's diplomatic and gentle encouragement of the congregation in Corinth to pick up where they had left off in gathering benevolence funds for the Jerusalem church. Although we won't be able to stop for long at individual verses, we will be learning several key principles that apply to Christian, and congregational, giving.

Let's first set the stage: from early on, the congregation in Jerusalem had suffered extreme poverty on account of the faith. Though they numbered in the thousands, these Christ-confessors came to be ostracized socially and economically; ecclesiastically and nationally they were without a name and a place. Imagine the stress put upon business and family, where relationships were torn and roots were severed.

Already in 1 Corinthians, Paul had mentioned plans for organizing a collection for these Jerusalem saints (see 1 Cor. 16:1-4). And from the passage we are studying now, it appears that the Macedonian churches (in Philippi, Thessalonica and Berea) had responded generously to his appeal for funds. After writing this epistle, Paul wrote the church in Rome about his intention to bring the gathered collection to Jerusalem, 'for the poor among the saints' (see Rom. 15:25-27).

In our passage the apostle deals with the Corinthians' participation in this contribution. From verses 10-11 we learn that though they had begun the project, they had allowed it to lapse, probably under the influence of false apostles interested in diverting the funds to their own pockets.

With pastoral diplomacy, Paul begins by pointing to the example of the Macedonian churches. Here, too, conversion to Christ had resulted in poverty and affliction, as businessmen lost customers and families were fractured. But in spite of meager resources, God had given these believers the grace of open-handed generosity. Divine grace was displayed in their liberality amid crushing poverty and suffering (see verse 2). Here we find an important principle for Christian giving: *the grace of true generosity is not dependent on adequacy of means.* The supreme measure of this generosity is the fullness not of our hands, but of our hearts. (*Question 1*)

This is but one more example of the overall theme of our study of 2 Corinthians: 'gospel power magnified through human weakness.' What religion can compare, what lifestyle can match, and what power can approach, the joy-in-suffering and the generosity-amid-poverty described in verse 2?

This Macedonian generosity is characterized further in verses 3-5. These believers gave not simply according to their ability, but even *beyond* their ability—that is: they gave more than they could really afford! Their giving consisted, we read, in 'the fellowship of the ministering to the saints' (verse 4). And because these believers had first given *themselves* to the Lord and His cause, their financial gifts followed as a natural consequence (verse 5). Giving until it hurts . . . giving as an exercise of the communion of the saints . . . and open hands that proceed from hearts sacrificed to the LORD—these are the principles and characteristics of *Christian* generosity.

In view of this Macedonian example, Paul had urged his pastoral assistant, Titus, to finish the collection work begun in Corinth. It seems that Titus had visited Corinth twice before the writing of this letter, and that he had started collecting for the Jerusalem relief fund even before 1 Corinthians had been written.

Notice, in verse 6, that the apostle speaks of Titus completing 'this (act of) grace' among the Corinthians as well. Here is another important clue about Christian giving, namely, that as the *source* of generosity is God's grace, so too the *expression* of generosity is itself a divine grace. Both are of God! As a demonstration of gratitude, Christian generosity is the return of grace. This spiritual cycle resembles the natural cycle of precipitation and evaporation.

Following Christ in sacrificing for others (read 8:8-12)

Study how the apostle seeks, by means of 'affectionate diplomacy,' to incite the congregation to affectionate generosity. Realizing that sacrifice cannot be compelled, he coaxes them to obey God like children rather than slaves. (*Question 2*)

He has explained and praised the example of the Macedonian churches, not to generate a spirit of rivalry or competition, but to spur the Corinthians to self-examination. If exercising the communion of the saints requires benevolence toward fellow-believers, how well are they doing?

But an even better incentive toward liberality is the example of Jesus Christ. It was His self-giving on behalf of rebellious sinners that should convince the Corinthians to give generously. This Jesus Christ emptied Himself, humbled Himself, becoming a servant—more: He was made to be *sin* (2 Cor. 5:21)—all of which led Him to the cross (see Phil. 2:6-8).

But the crowning touch of the apostle's pastoral diplomacy appears in the words '*for your sakes.*' Jesus Christ didn't renounce wealth and glory in order to make a moral or cultural 'statement.' Rather, He voluntarily entered a state of humiliation—which means, remember, that He was counted *guilty* before God's law; it does *not* mean simply that 'He gave up a lot' to 'come down here to be with us'—in order effectively to accomplish the redemption of God's elect. This is part of what Paul means by adding, '. . . that you through His poverty might become rich' (verse 9). Though He became poor, Christ never lost His riches, for His glory and deity were always present in His humanity. Instead, His poverty and self-emptying have enriched believers, for through the shedding of His blood their sins have been atoned for.

Now that he has shown them their Savior as the best example and inducement for giving, Paul doesn't continue 'preaching' at the congregation. With fatherly tone and warm appreciation for what had once flowed from their hearts, he gently prods them to finish the job. A year earlier their desire and readiness had been enthusiastic. Instead of complaining about their lapse, he pushes forward with a kindly nudge: 'Go ahead, now. C'mon, just do it!'

Equality as the goal of communion (read 8:13-15)

Repeatedly the apostle takes great pains to explain his motives and goals to his readers. Verses 13-15 are another example of this apostolic self-explanation. Why does he explain himself so often? Perhaps to answer ahead of time the criticisms that might arise in the congregation from false leaders or questioning church members.

You can imagine the criticisms, can't you? 'What's Paul trying to do—put *us* in the poor house too? Why should we send our charity away when we could use it right here at home? And besides, who's going to help us when we fall on hard times?'

Sounds like our own day and age, doesn't it!

Another idea that sounds surprisingly modern is Paul's desire for *equality* among congregations. But don't let the 'sound' fool you. Be very careful at this point not to import into our passage the modern notion that equality means *sameness*. Paul wants to encourage here not an equalization of property, but the exercise of reciprocal benevolence. It is true that all those in Christ, no matter of what gender or socio-economic class, are one (Gal. 3:28). But they are *not* thereby the same. *Unity* should never be confused with *uniformity*.

This is confirmed by his appeal to the Old Testament example of gathering manna, mentioned in Exodus 16:18: 'So when they measured it by omers, he who gathered much had nothing left over, and he who gathered little had no lack. Every man had gathered according to each one's need.' *Equality meant sufficiency*. This principle, illustrated from the church's Old Testament history, can now spur the saints in Corinth to help those in Jerusalem. Elsewhere Paul put it this way: 'Therefore, as we have opportunity, let us do good to all, especially to those who are of the household of faith' (Gal. 6:10). (*Question 3*)

Arrangements for collecting the gift (read 8:16-24)

Fund-raising is a delicate business. It requires tact and sensitivity to approach people with the goal of receiving money *from them*, while convincing them of your care *for them*.

The person Paul appointed to do this, however, was a missionary-colleague whose love for the Corinthian congregation was as deep as it was open. He volunteered to go fund-raising in Corinth, so eager was he to 'prove' their love for the gospel and for fellow-believers.

Titus did not travel alone. Two other brothers, well-attested and respected among the churches, accompanied him on this mission of mercy. From the passage itself we cannot be sure who these two were. Speculations point to no fewer than eleven possibilities! One of these companions was probably Luke, a frequent companion and colleague of Paul.

Maintaining the churches' trust and respect was important, for, as Calvin reminds us, 'there is nothing which is more apt to lay one open to sinister imputations than the handling of public money.' Paul wished to steer clear of any impropriety in the gathering and administering of this gift (see verse 20).

In verse 23 the apostle furnishes, as it were, the credentials attesting to the reliability of the fund-raising committee. Titus was well-known as Paul's fellow worker. The other two colleagues are (1) brothers in the faith, and (2) messengers or representatives of the churches, which churches (3) bring glory to Christ by their faithful lifestyle and witness.

Finally, in verse 24, the apostle gently appeals to the congregation to make good his boasting about them. 'Show these representatives, and through them, all the churches, your love and generosity by opening your hands and filling theirs.' Show them, in other words, that God's grace can be multiplied and magnified through the exercise of the communion of saints. Know yourselves bound to employ your gifts readily and cheerfully for the advantage and salvation of other members! (*Questions 4 and 5*)

Questions for Reflection and Reply

1. Mention ways in which this spiritual principle can form your giving habits. Is any Christian ever too poor to give? How can we teach giving as a spiritual exercise?

2. Why would God rather have us relate to Him as children than as slaves? What is the difference, with respect to our giving? How can we ensure that we give as children rather than as slaves?

3. 'From each according to his ability, to each according to his need.' This is the slogan of Marxism. How does Paul's discussion of *equality* differ from the ideals of Marxism or modern socialism?

4. Review the discussion of 2 Cor. 8:16-24, and use it to evaluate the fund-raising techniques of institutions, agencies and organizations you are currently supporting. Is a 'faith-promise pledge' biblical?

5. Should Christians support *para-church* organizations (not governed by, or accountable to, any church)? Why (not)?

Lesson 10

2 Corinthians 9:1-15

Ministerial Encouragement for the Communion of the Saints (2)

Memory Verse: 'But this I say: He who sows sparingly will also reap sparingly, and he who sows bountifully will also reap bountifully. So let each one give as he purposes in his heart, not grudgingly or of necessity; for God loves a cheerful giver. And God is able to make all grace abound toward you, that you, always having all sufficiency in all things, may have an abundance for every good work.'

2 Corinthians 9:6-8

Once more: arrangements for the collection (read 9:1-5)

The Corinthians' initial readiness to contribute to the needs of Jerusalem believers was the subject of Paul's boasting to the Macedonians. In fact, the Corinthians' early zeal had aroused the Macedonian Christians to give so freely and sacrificially.

However, this Corinthian readiness had not yet matured into performance. And that was the reason for the three-man committee sent ahead (see 8:16-23), whose mandate included raising the promised funds. You see, Paul was intending to visit Corinth shortly, taking along some fellow-believers from Macedonia. The apostle and his companions risked being embarrassed if the Corinthians failed to make good on their intention to share in the collection for the Jerusalem saints.

Interestingly, the apostle explains his motive further in verse 5, and at the same time builds a bridge to what follows: 'Therefore I thought it necessary to exhort the brethren to go to you ahead of time, and prepare your generous gift beforehand, which you had previously promised, that it may be ready *as a matter of generosity and not as a grudging obligation.*' The King James Version renders the italicized clause, 'as a matter of bounty, and not as of covetousness.' The notion here is that if the apostle and his Macedonian companions were to come to Corinth without those preparatory arrangements, the congregation would be caught unprepared and would be inclined to give its gift from a sense of religious extortion. Because their hearts would not have been in their giving, their 'generosity' would proceed from covetousness—giving, indeed, but not really wanting to do so.

The manner of grace-filled giving (read 9:6-7)

Generosity, the apostle has been explaining, is a gift, an ability proceeding from divine grace. Therefore, it should reflect the character and essence of that grace. God's grace is limitless, abundant, free-flowing. Our giving should be like that.

To make his point, Paul employs a metaphor: giving is like sowing seed in a field. This comparison teaches us the significant lesson that, just as when a seed is sown, it is not lost, but only hidden temporarily from view, so too the gifts we give for the Lord's work, if they proceed from a gracious heart, have power to multiply unto a rich harvest.

All of this echoes the Old Testament, where centuries earlier this wisdom about generosity had been formulated in three related proverbs:

There is one who scatters, yet increases more;
And there is one who withholds more than is right,
But it leads to poverty.

The generous soul will be made rich,
And he who waters will also be watered himself.

The people will curse him who withholds grain,
But blessing will be on the head of him who sells it.

(Prov. 11:24-26)

Not only do we reap *what* we sow, but we reap *in the same measure* that we sow. And this measure is judged not first in terms of quantity, but in terms of the quality of our hearts. Are our hearts more like a dripping faucet, or an open river of blessing toward others? Must our hands be pried open because our hearts are pinched tight by the fear of parting with our hard-earned money? Or are we, like the Macedonian Christians, in danger of giving away more than we can really afford? (*Question 1*)

Christian giving is first of all a heart matter. This is made especially clear in verse 7: 'So let each one give as he purposes in his heart, not

64

grudgingly or of necessity; for God loves a cheerful giver.' With regard to this collection for benevolence, Paul isn't interested in setting a 'budgeted amount' or a 'quota' for the Corinthian believers, for he realizes that giving in terms of such an external standard can so often proceed from duty instead of delight, from the grudging obligation commonly associated with 'paying bills.'

The real mark of free, open-handed giving is *cheerfulness*. The giver ought to find pleasure in giving. Giving should be an exhilarating experience, because it generates spiritual happiness within donor and recipient alike. The standard for giving, therefore, is the intention of a heart moved by grace, saturated with love for God and the fellowship. (*Question 2*)

From one miracle to another (read 9:8-9)

From description Paul moves to promise-filled prediction. This divine grace is able both to spur believers to generosity and to supply their needs in all things. Notice how comprehensive *God's* generosity is toward His children, expressed by the apostle with a heaping-up of 'alls': 'And God is able to make *all* grace abound toward you, that you, *always* having *all* sufficiency in *all* things, may have an abundance for *every* good work' (verse 8). If that confidence doesn't make us cheerful givers, nothing will! God's *miracle of harvest*, whereby the seed sown in generosity is multiplied in blessing upon others, is exceeded only by the miracle *of inexhaustible resources!* Generous Christians always have more than enough for their own needs! That was demonstrated to the widow of Zarephath and her son, as they ministered to God's servant, Elijah (see 1 Kings 17:8-16). And the same promise holds for God's children in every age.

Reaching back into his Bible once more, the apostle quotes from a poem pronouncing a beatitude upon 'the man who fears the LORD, who delights greatly in His commandments' (Ps. 112:1). Such a person 'has dispersed abroad, he has given to the poor; his righteousness endures forever; his horn will be exalted with honor' (Ps. 112:9).

Generosity toward fellow-believers, you see, is a matter of right-eousness. It was commanded by God through Moses (see Lev. 25:35 and Deut. 15:7-11). And here in 2 Corinthians, Paul continues the charitable teaching of the law, the prophets and the psalms, while at the same time going beyond by appealing to the added incentive of being recipients of God's grace in Jesus Christ, God's own 'indescribable gift' toward us (see 2 Cor. 9:15). The righteousness of these Corinthian believers must—and *can!*—match that taught in the Old Testament cove-nant administration. Moreover, this righteousness consists of kindness toward co-believers, concern for the poor and afflicted, preached repeatedly by the prophets and redemptively by our Savior (see Matt. 6:1-4). *(Question 3)*

Divine grace magnified through grace-filled giving (read 9:10-14)

Would you care to see still more of God's grace? It's all summarized for us in verse 10. We've already learned that *generosity* is a gift of divine grace, and that the *miracle of harvest* comes from heaven itself. Paul now prays that the God who provides natural seed for sowing *and* bread for eating will multiply the spiritual seed sown through the Corinthian congregation's generosity. This spiritual seed will, under God's gracious rain and sunshine, produce a harvest of righteousness, enriching the Corinthians for all kinds of liberality, and producing through the apostle and his colleagues hearty thanksgiving to God.

God's grace grows, as it were, and spreads out like a garden vine, full of luscious fruit which itself contains seeds for another planting and harvest. The cycle of grace imitates the cycle of nature, or perhaps better stated: the 'laws' of redemption mirror those of creation.

This ministry of mercy is an exercise of *the communion of the saints.* According to verse 12, its effect is twofold: it supplies the material needs of the saints, and generates thanksgiving toward God. The second is the aim of the first, while the first is surely an important avenue toward the second. Here 'the material' and 'the spiritual' are joined together, as believers place 'nature' into the service of 'grace.' This is the profound mystery lying at the heart of our calling 'to employ [our] gifts readily and cheerfully for the advantage and *salvation* of other members' *(Heidelberg Catechism,* QA 55). Christians are called to place themselves, their possessions, their talents and abilities, all in service to the *salvation* of other church members. Not that we *cooperate* with Jesus Christ in 'redeeming' people or activities or culture, but rather that we, along with our possessions temporarily entrusted to us by God, are serviceable to Christ's final redemption of them one day.

As if looking ahead to the time when the Jerusalem congregation would receive their gift with rejoicing, Paul sees the church in Palestine glorifying God for the Corinthians' obedience to the gospel of Christ, and for their liberality.

Don't let this little note escape your attention. Remember that most of the Jerusalem believers were *Jews*, while most of the Corinthian Christians were *Gentiles.* Proof of their common confession and allegiance to *Christ* (notice that Paul omits our Savior's personal name, and uses only His official name, Messiah-Anointed) lay in the sacrificial benevolence given by the Corinthians and received by the Jerusalemites. More than that, it would spur the Jerusalem Christians to pray for and love their Gentile brothers and sisters in Corinth.

Generating all of these results, and more, this collection would be an expression of true unity and catholicity among Christ's churches in every place. *(Questions 4 and 5)*

The Source of every good and perfect gift (read 9:15)

So moved is the apostle by thinking of these things that he ends with an outburst of praise, a one-line doxology: 'Thanks be to God for His indescribable gift!'

This gift is Jesus Christ Himself, God's only-begotten Son, His beloved Son.

Indeed, who can really describe God's heart, the depth of His generosity, the cost of His sacrifice, the dimensions of His love?

There remains only one application: 'Beloved, if God so loved us, we also ought to love one another' (1 John 4:11).

Questions for Reflection and Reply

1. Do you agree that Christian giving is first of all a matter of 'how,' and not of 'how much'? Can we really separate these two? Some church members decide how much to give each week on the basis of an agreed-upon, per member amount (the total financial needs are divided by the number of members or families); following this method, each member or family gives the same amount. Is this a good method? Why (not)?

2. Mention ways to improve our cheerfulness in giving.

3. If our righteousness must and can match that taught in the Old Testament, discuss:
   Why is tithing the Christian's required *minimum?*

   What should the tithe be a tenth of?

   Why don't many Christians give at least a tithe?

4. Review 2 Corinthians 9:10-14, along with our lesson discussion of these verses, and explain how the following are affected by grace-filled giving:
Our praying

Church unity

Christ's redemption of others

5. May we give with a view to the consequences or effects of our giving on others? Why (not)? If so, what are some dangers of giving in terms of consequences or results?

Lesson 11

2 Corinthians 10:1-18

Congregational Critics Answered with Ministerial Authority

Memory Verse: 'For the weapons of our warfare are not carnal but mighty in God for pulling down strongholds, casting down arguments and every high thing that exalts itself against the knowledge of God, bringing every thought into captivity to the obedience of Christ, and being ready to punish all disobedience when your obedience is fulfilled.'

2 Corinthians 10:4-6

2 Corinthians 10-13: Self-defense against false apostles

We have come, in our study of this epistle, to an important turning point in the apostle's writing. Chapters 10-13 are tied together by the common thread of apostolic self-defense. Careful reading will alert us to the charges being leveled against Paul and to his responses, both forthright and subtle. Patient study will repay us with rich biblical insights about ministerial identity and leadership expectations.

Because a study like this cannot spend time explaining choices of interpretation, we must suffice with a brief characterization of Paul's opponents in the Corinthian congregation. These people were, first, not native to the church, but outsiders, something strongly hinted in 10:13-15, 11:4, and 12:11. They were latecomers, intruders, leaders who had gained prominence and authority, in part by dragging down the authority and leadership of Paul. Second, it is clear from 2 Corinthians 11:22 that these misleaders were Jews, probably Judaizers trying to seduce Gentile and Jewish believers back under the yoke of Old Testament ritual.

Meeting opposition with Christlike meekness (read 10:1-2)

With more than a bit of irony Paul takes up the charge being circulated among the Corinthians. Their criticism? Paul was an inconsistent minister. His detractors were spreading the idea that, although from a distance he could write letters that stung with rebuke, in person he was weak and ineffectual.

Part of this irony lies in the apostle's style. Instead of blasting away with *commands* ringing with apostolic authority (as his critics would have expected), this pastor-apostle *appeals* on the basis of the meekness and gentleness of Christ. The words 'of Christ' are crucial here. The Corinthians had been confusing Paul's personal meekness with weakness, his gentleness with spinelessness. By responding in terms of the character and teaching of Christ, the apostle suggests that his opponents have no grasp of these fundamental Christian virtues of meekness and gentleness, which our Lord demonstrated in His own ministry. Instead of meekness, they emphasized oratorical prowess; in place of gentleness, worldly shrewdness and manipulation. (*Question 1*)

Paul's appeal contains a warning (verse 2): when the occasion called for it, he could be bold in person. There are 'some' in the congregation who, if they do not repent, will experience the apostle's boldness full force. Their sin is an unwarranted, incorrect opinion about Paul's ministry. They talk him down as if he 'walked according to the flesh,' governed by self-interest and concerned only for his position among the Corinthians.

Destroying opposition with spiritual weapons (read 10:3-6)

Apostolic, Christ-like meekness should never be equated with wimpiness. For in the very next section, Paul warns these Corinthians, to whom he had just appealed with the gentleness of Christ, that he has been sent out on a search-and-destroy mission. Look here: pastoral kindness *can* be coupled with spiritual aggression!

Although the 'flesh' is Paul's sphere of activity, that does not mean that his methods are dictated by the 'flesh.' In the New Testament, 'flesh' can mean: (1) the physical flesh covering our bones; (2) the old way of life, or sinful nature, as a controlling principle (Rom. 8:9); (3) worldly standards of behavior. Here, in 2 Corinthians 10:2-4, Paul defends himself against the charge of following a worldly spirituality in his ministry.

Notice the easy shift of metaphors, from walking to making war. Not only is the Christian *life* a battle (see Eph. 6:11ff; 1 Tim. 1:18; 2 Tim. 2:3ff.; 4:7; and 2 Cor. 6:7), but so too is the Christian *ministry!*

How dangerous it is, in wartime, to pick up and use the wrong weapons! The church and her leaders are always tempted to counter the world's persistent challenges by using weapons forged in the world's foundries—weapons like wisdom, eloquence, entertainment, efficiency, and so on. None of these is wrong in itself, but all are unusable as weapons to accomplish the apostle's spiritual purpose. He wants to pull down strongholds, to cast down arguments, to take every thought prisoner for Christ, to punish all disobedience.

His military objective is that the gospel of Christ overpower rebellious human *intellect* and *will*. The weapons of his ministry are designed to demolish the way people think, their sinful thought patterns and those mental structures according to which they rebel against God. These weapons destroy all those human pretensions erected to shut out the knowledge of God. Rebellion against God is sometimes disguised as intellectual doubt and skepticism, and often surfaces as an intellectual independence that is so full of itself as to be unable to bend in worship.

How well-suited, then, are the minister's weapons: truth, righteousness, peace, faith, salvation, the Word of God, and prayer. All are bestowed in and with the gospel of Christ-crucified; none is dependent on human gimmickry or ingenuity. (*Question 2*)

The apostle is unwilling to stop halfway. So 'wound up' is he in the calling to preach and make war with the gospel, that he warns of the impending punishment of disobedience in the congregation. Competent military leaders know that no war is really won until the cause that occasioned the fighting is removed. The inability, or unwillingness, to root out the cause of fighting (through proper discipline) renders the church susceptible to continued attack and disruption by the gospel's enemies.

Self-defense without self-exaltation (read 10:7-11)

It is quite impossible for both individual believers and Christian congregations to avoid judging—that is: evaluating teaching and conduct. *How* that judgment is rendered is quite important, as our Lord taught us (Matt. 7:1-6). *That* we must judge is beyond dispute.

If this is so, then we need to be committed to making biblical judgments biblically. The *content* as well as the *manner* of our judging must be according to standards found in God's Word.

Paul's critics in Corinth were not practicing biblical judgment.

Two criticisms about the apostle were being circulated. First, his opponents alleged that Paul did not belong to Christ in the same, superior, intimate way that they did. Second, people were saying that, like a dog that barks at a distance but cowers when confronted, Paul wielded a mighty pen, but was mousy in person. In a word: Paul was a phony.

Now, how does a minister respond to such charges? To defend himself is to contradict the very point he wishes to prove, namely: that his person is not the center of his ministry. (*Question 3*)

Very carefully, the apostle defends his position in Christ ('just as he is Christ's, even so we are Christ's,' verse 7), and explains the purpose of his apostolic authority, which was given not for self-promotion, but for the edification or building up of the congregation (verse 8). Yes, this building up may at times require stern rebuke, inflexible discipline, and confrontational judgment. *But these are built into the very gospel itself!*

Once again, the apostle places before the congregation, as a standard for judgment and evaluation of the preacher, this truth: the exercise of ministerial leadership must fit the content of the gospel.

And his leadership does. To be sure, he is flexible where the gospel permits flexibility (circumcising Timothy, but not Titus, for example). Yet, superficial observers, who will not or cannot discern the underlying principles driving his action, charge him with inconsistency. With a veiled threat, Paul declares in verse 11: 'I'm consistent, alright. Just wait till I come. Then you'll see that I can be just as bold in person as I am with the pen!'

The core of ministerial identity (read 10:12-18)

Someone applying for a college teaching position might compose a long, flowery letter of self-recommendation called a *curriculum vitae* (literally, 'course of life'). Details of birth, marriage and family are followed by a list of educational accomplishments, titles of books and articles written, memberships in professional organizations, and the like.

Reading verses 12-18, one quickly surmises that the apostle Paul would have refused to write a *curriculum vitae*.

Earlier (2 Cor. 3:3-4), we saw that the Corinthian congregation was the only credential needed to establish the apostle's authenticity. Why? Because they were living proof of the transforming gospel of Christ! Now, Paul complains that the false teachers are using the subjective, arbitrary standard *of themselves* to measure and recommend themselves to the congregation. These self-promoters use one another as references, appealing to each other's abilities, pedigree and training to establish their own credibility.

For Paul, by contrast, it is living the gospel of Christ, by sharing in

His sufferings and conforming to His character, that validates the minister's authenticity.

How many people in churches today fall for the same folly of applying to their minister the fickle standards of performance drawn from the arenas of politics and entertainment (not unrelated spheres, by the way!)? Like infants more fascinated with the wrapping paper than its contents, many church members seek style over substance. And how many ministers today are attempting to fashion their labor in terms of these constantly shifting standards? How can these 'professionals' end up saying so little, but saying it so well? (*Question 4*)

Changing to a metaphor drawn from geography (regional boundaries) or athletics (lane markings), Paul insists that because he was authorized by Christ to bring the gospel to Corinth and beyond, the false teachers in Corinth were guilty of trespassing, overrunning the boundaries divinely appointed for him. By arriving in Corinth after him and seducing people away from the gospel, these misleaders lived like parasites off the evangelistic labors of the apostle. They were ecclesiastical poachers.

Not self-commendation, but the LORD's commendation, is what gospel ministers should seek.

Spiritual, ministerial boasting is a troublesome sport. It quickly degenerates into one-up-manship. Commending oneself generally diverts from praising the Lord. Of all this Paul is painfully aware. The crucial distinction between Paul and his opponents in Corinth was their respective answers to the question: *Whose approval do we seek?* That, of course, is the central issue in all Christian living, in every moral decision, in each church dispute. But in terms of this passage and its direct application, the answer to this question lies at the core of the minister's identity, and the congregation's expectations of the minister.

Questions for Reflection and Reply

1. Show from the life of Christ that meekness and firmness, love and anger, are compatible.

2. Read Romans 12:1-3, 2 Corinthians 10:5 and 11:3. Why does *thinking* have priority over *feeling* in the Christian scheme of things? What are some results of religion governed by or centered on feelings?

3. Identify and explain the biblical steps that should be followed in processing a valid criticism of a minister. And how must one who persists in voicing an invalid criticism be handled biblically?

4. Identify some of those fickle standards of performance drawn from politics and entertainment and applied to the minister. Why are they necessarily *shifting* standards? What's inherently dangerous about applause in the worship service?

Lesson 12

2 Corinthians 11:1-15

Congregational Critics Answered with Godly Jealousy

Memory Verse: 'For I am jealous for you with godly jealousy. For I have betrothed you to one husband, that I may present you as a chaste virgin to Christ. But I fear, lest somehow, as the serpent deceived Eve by his craftiness, so your minds may be corrupted from the simplicity that is in Christ.'

2 Corinthians 11:2-3

A spiritual father pleads for understanding (read 11:1-6)

From our previous study we learned that 'not he who commends himself is approved, but whom the Lord commends' (2 Cor. 10:18). Self-commendation is unsuitable for a preacher of Christ, and embarrassing for the apostle Paul. With loving concern for the spiritual welfare of his Corinthian children, he begs their indulgence of his apparent 'foolishness' as he sets out to defend his reputation against criticisms being circulated in the congregation.

His motive, simply stated, is spiritual jealousy for them (verse 2). So intense is his love for the Corinthian congregation that it burns with *godly* jealousy, the protective, directive affection of a father for his daughter. Paul had begotten this spiritual daughter through the gospel (1 Cor. 9:1f.; 4:15), and had exercised the father's ancient right of betrothing her in marriage to an approved bridegroom: Christ Himself. The wedding day is approaching, but in the meantime, this spiritual father desires to keep his spiritual daughter pure and chaste for presentation to the Groom. (*Question 1*)

But the apostle has been hearing reports of his 'daughter' playing around with other lovers, seduced away from her affection for her Betrothed. Notice in verse 3 how this paternal apprehension is expressed: 'But I fear, lest somehow, as the serpent deceived Eve by his craftiness, so your *minds* may be corrupted from the simplicity that is in

Christ.' Eve fell because she was not wholly devoted to God, and therefore her mind was seduced by the devil's cunning. Paul is implying that these false apostles are servants of Satan—deceitful and cunning in their motives and doctrine. In fact, later in verses 13 and 15, he states the charge explicitly: these false teachers masquerade as if they are from Christ, even as Satan masquerades as an angel of light. (*Question 2*)

The basic issue is exposed at the end of verse 4: *you people are too tolerant!* If somebody comes preaching another Jesus, offering another spirit, a different gospel, 'you put up with it easily enough!' Even the heretical Judaizers, who wanted to crawl back to Old Testament ceremonial ritual, used Jesus' name, appealed to the Bible, and claimed certain spiritual realities consistent with the gospel. Nevertheless, theirs was *another* (that is: different) Jesus.

Commenting on this verse, Donald Carson observes that 'the Christian church needs a little more both of Paul's discernment and intolerance. Like the ancient Corinthians, we too are sometimes deceived. Provided there is fluent talk about Jesus, gospel, truth, Christian living, and spiritual experience, combined with effective, self-confident leadership, we seldom ask if it is the same Jesus as the one presented in the Scriptures, or if the gospel being presented squares with the apostolic gospel.'

Ask yourself: Is it a biblical Jesus who promises heaven, but says nothing of hell? Is the Jesus who offers people prosperity and health the Jesus of the Bible? Is it a biblical Jesus who needs His sacrifices supplemented by our ceremonies and works in order to redeem?

Another reason why Paul's readers should indulge him as he defends himself is that he is not inferior to those 'super apostles' who are going around the congregation criticizing him (verses 5-6). He might not have employed the flourish of rhetorical style, or the persuasive arguments of philosophy, both so common in those days. Paul's self-defense is simple and straightforward: he had communicated the truth perfectly clearly. You didn't have to guess what he meant, or disagree about where he stood. Everybody in the congregation knew. We sense underlying his words an implicit accusation that the Corinthians had fallen for the outward blandishments—the style and pizazz—of these false teachers.

Financial and ecclesiastical parasites (read 11:7-12)

In the ancient world, traveling teachers were not generally supported by their own manual labor, but by the tuition they charged their students. The more famous the teacher was, the higher tuition he could afford to charge. Much like today's lecture-circuit speakers, the orator's status was judged by the size of his fee!

Although Paul acknowledged the principle that one who preaches the gospel has the right to live by the gospel (1 Cor. 9:7-12a), he occasionally refused payment so that the message of the gospel (*free grace*) could be reinforced by the method of its preacher (see 1 Cor. 9:16-18). So the apostle had refused financial support from the congregation when he labored in Corinth. (*Question 3*)

The unkind conclusion which the Corinthians drew had been carefully framed by the false teachers. This guy Paul must not be much of an apostle if he gets no money for his work. 'His message is worth what you paid him,' the Corinthians were being told.

Paul responds with three arguments.

First, his refusal of support was self-denial, renouncing his rights for their sake. How can they criticize him for that?! Paul's willingness to support himself by manual labor permitted him to begin immediately building the church in Corinth, rather than having to wait for support from other churches. Moreover, if Paul was wrong for practicing such self-denial, what about Jesus Christ, whose example he was following?! The Corinthians had absorbed, perhaps unwittingly, the poisonous idea that gospel ministry—its methods of financing and persuasion—is really no more than showmanship, people-centered performance for applause. Paul didn't fit their mold, because *Christ* didn't really fit their expectations!

His second argument explains his strategy. He had depended for his support on other churches, especially from Macedonia (2 Cor. 11:9a; Acts 18:5; Phil. 4:15). He 'robbed' other churches, so to speak, to support his ministry in Corinth. And his practice would continue (verse 9). 'As long as they were going to weigh him by the size of his take, as long as they were utilizing the standards of the world to evaluate message and messenger alike, so long was Paul unwilling to reinforce their pagan approach by receiving anything from their hand' (Carson).

So distorted was their perception of Paul that they needed a virtual oath from his pen that the motive of his self-denial was his love for their welfare. Can't they see the method and motives of Christ Himself in the apostle's conduct toward them? Are they so blind?!

The final explanation for his strategy appears in verse 12. The apostle wishes to cut the ground from under his critics. His ministry is 'free' because its message communicates free grace. Their methods betray their motives: as parasites they live off the church, sucking her blood as they poison her body. They actively work against the gospel in the name of the gospel.

The real problem exposed (read 11:13-15)

There is an old German proverb that says, 'Tell me with whom you are fighting, and I'll tell you who you are.' A person's intellectual and religious commitment is determined as much by what one opposes as by what he accepts. If fighting for the truth and against heresy embarrasses us, that may be the clearest indication of how far we've left the apostolic gospel.

'The appeal to limitless toleration—not just toleration of the other chap's right to be wrong, but toleration pushed so far one can never say that anything or anyone is wrong—presupposes the greatest evil is to hold a strong conviction that certain things are true and their contraries are false' (Carson). Behind this view of toleration lies the assumption that certainty in religious matters is impossible. Nobody can really know what the Bible teaches about _____ (you fill in the blank); so for anyone to say that *he* knows is to be arrogant, authoritarian and intolerant. (*Questions 4 and 5*)

Until now, the apostle's descriptions of his critics in the congregation have been only indirect. But here, in 11:13-15, the picture is painted in bold color. These false apostles are servants of Satan, and like the devil, disguise themselves as teachers of truth. The way that Satan works is to deceive—that is his stock in trade, his mark of distinction, his *modus operandi.* And among those who become his victims are they who believe themselves to be sophisticated, who shun 'simple' faith and obedience. (*Question 6*)

Diabolical—devilish, demonic. That's what these false leaders are. And their end will fit their actions. Just as Paul is finally and eternally answerable to the God who called and sent him to preach, so too are these impostors going to be judged and punished for their church-wrecking and sheep-scattering work. Notice, then, the apostle's subtle irony: these false teachers (Judaizers) who deny the grace of the gospel by insisting on the merit of works, will finally be judged according to their own works! They will reap what they have sown!

Questions for Reflection and Reply

1. Mention some features of sinful human jealousy that distinguish it from godly jealousy.

2. How can Satan corrupt our *minds?* Why are things like music, movies or television so useful in corrupting people's minds?

3. Which is a better method: that missionaries raise their own funds, or that they depend on 'home churches' for financial support? Why?

4. Surely we don't (and can't) know everything with equal certainty. Here are two examples: we don't know very much about what heaven will be like, and opinions differed even among Reformers about remarriage after divorce. How do we know which differences must or may be tolerated, and which ones not? How would you distinguish biblical toleration from unbiblical toleration?

5. Paul complains that the Corinthian believers were too tolerant. What should they have done instead? Why is it often more difficult to discipline false teachers in the church than other members?

6. How can we spot someone disguised as a servant of Christ? What should we listen and look for?

Lesson 13

2 Corinthians 11:16-33

Answering Fools According to Their Folly

Memory Verse: 'If I must boast, I will boast in the things which concern my infirmity.'   *2 Corinthians 11:30*

Apostolic 'foolishness' in reply to false teachers (read 11:16-21)

We have been learning, in the preceding lessons, just how sensitive and difficult pastoral self-defense can be. None was more aware of this than the Christ-glorifying, grace-preaching apostle Paul. He knew that self-*defense* can easily slide into self-*recommendation*.

In 2 Corinthians 11:16, he resumes the theme announced in verse 1: he is willing to act like a fool in boasting about his own credentials, if that's what it takes to win the Corinthian believers away from their love-affair with false teachers.

We are tipped off in verse 17 that Paul is affecting or pretending to adopt the style of his opponents: 'What I speak, I speak not according to the Lord, but as it were, foolishly, in this confidence of boasting.' This was not Christ's style at all! Paul wanted so much to imitate Christ in his ministry among the Corinthians. They should have seen and remembered that. But, alas, he must now temporarily adopt the style of his adversaries, stooping to their level in order to gain a hearing.

His first salvo aims some biting criticism at the Corinthian congregation. In verses 19-20, Paul uses irony tinged with sarcasm to remind these Corinthians that they 'suffer fools gladly'! So undiscerning and tolerant, so openminded and naive are they that Paul's temporary, pretended foolishness shouldn't upset them one bit. In fact, their seemingly limitless toleration had permitted these false leaders to manipulate, exploit, intimidate and humiliate the congregation. For the intruders had located, and then taken over, positions of influence in the congregation, enabling them to seize control of the church.

With stinging irony Paul adds, 'To our shame, I say that we were too weak for that!'

These believers had fallen in love with the 'style' of worldly wisdom and efficiency. Good speaking ability, friendly personality, community involvement, snappy dresser—these were the measure of their leaders! At the same time, their love and respect for the meekness, gentleness and servanthood of Christ, demonstrated among them by His workman Paul, had grown cold and lifeless. They had chosen flash, splash and dash, and dismissed as nothing more than irrelevant 'weakness' the devoted, plodding, unspectacular commitment out of which the church had been born. (*Questions 1 and 2*)

How painful these words of rebuke are, directed toward believers at home *in the church* with the world's ways! 'The wound to the Corinthians' ego, like the wound of the surgeon, is designed to remove a particularly vicious cancer. Few malignancies are more dangerous than arrogance fed by ignorance, or triumphalism nurtured by a secular mind' (Donald Carson, *From Triumphalism to Maturity*).

Fools answered according to their folly (read 11:22-29)

The apostle begins his boast, then, with four rhetorical questions, tuned to the pitch being hummed by his opponents: Are they full-blooded Jews? I am too. Are they members of God's special people? So am I. Do they claim the rights and privileges of being Abraham's children? So do I. Do they dare to claim to be servants of Christ? I even more.

With this last question, Paul in no way grants the truth of their claim to be serving Christ. In 2 Corinthians 11:13-15 he had described them as servants of Satan! Here he says simply: if you want to evaluate Christ's servants by sub-Christian standards, I have more credentials than they!

So now we expect Paul to do what many important people of his time did: to pull out his list of credentials, bragging of his accomplishments, tooting his own horn.

Notice what he details instead: imprisonments and floggings, along with their public humiliation and physical pain; Jewish scourgings (39 stripes); Roman beatings (unrestricted blows to any part of the body); and stoning. Paul suffered not only in connection with his message, but also en route to his mission fields: three shipwrecks, one of which apparently left him adrift until rescued; risking injury from nature and from robbers; endangered by Jew and Gentile alike, along crowded city streets and in the bandit-infested wilderness. Perhaps the most painful suffering occurred at the hands of 'false brothers,' people like the Judaizers who, although they confessed several 'essential' doctrines of

Christianity, had nonetheless compromised the message by addition or subtraction. Paul's list of 'accomplishments' concludes with references to exhaustion, sleeplessness, and living without the amenities of life.

As you read through this list in verses 23-28, observe the climax or capstone of Paul's trials: 'besides the other things, what comes upon me daily: my deep concern for all the churches.' All the churches, including those founded and pastored by the apostle himself, but surely the others as well, were the object of his constant concern and prayer. His ministry 'is not discharged with aloof detachment, but with flaming zeal, profound compassion, evangelistic fervor, and a father's heart' (Carson). This kind of ministry consumes the minister, exhausts his energy and emotions.

Paul empathized with the weak—those who, due to either physical or spiritual weakness, had a hard time making the grade. When, out of disregard for their faith-life, false teachers led them into sin, Paul burned with holy anger. Such abuse contradicted the gospel! (*Question 3*)

Have you noticed by now that Paul has turned the tables on these pretend-apostles? Rejecting *their* standards for what makes a good apostle-pastor, Paul brags instead about his *losses*, his *humiliations* and *defeats!* The value-systems employed by Paul and by the intruders are incompatible. Their ministerial profiles are antithetical.

Superb irony: boasting in weakness (read 11:30-33)

If the apostle comes close to boasting at all, it is in these verses. He brings up a shameful episode from days following his conversion: his escape from Damascus in a basket.

Before recounting the story, however, Paul identifies the quality of his boast. He boasts not in his strength and accomplishments, but in his weakness and shame. The truthfulness of his boast rests with the Lord Himself (verse 31).

But why report this seemingly innocuous incident as his crowning glory?

Part of our puzzlement may be due to having learned the story of Paul's escape from Damascus when we were in Sunday School, complete with flannelgraph and cut-outs! Acts 9:23-25 tells the story very concisely. But here, in 2 Corinthians 11:32-33, the apostle recalls the event with shame, likely because his disgraceful exit as a hunted criminal who had been dropped down in a smelly fish basket had shredded whatever pride remained in his heart. He will boast, along with the false apostles, if he must. But everyone in Corinth knew of the highest military honor, given to the first soldier *up and over* the enemy's wall.

The apostle's point—almost a parody of the pretensions of the false teachers in Corinth—is that *his* highest honor is to have been the first one *down* the wall!

Perhaps we can best summarize the lesson of our passage this way: for Christian leaders, pastors and believers, the source of our glory is not the war medals decorating our uniforms, but the war wounds scarring our bodies for Christ. The apostle's ability to glory in his weakness proceeded from God's grace, not from his naturally self-effacing personality. That is what he holds out to his Corinthian readers—and to us—as the only antidote for the poisonous leadership style of the world that so often infects the church. 'The solution to overblown self-esteem and self-eulogizing is neither an artificial self-loathing nor a valiant attempt to try harder. It is unconditional devotion to Jesus Christ' (Carson). Imitating Christ and suffering for Him are the key ingredients of a biblical style of ministry. This 'foolishness' embodies the 'foolish' message of the gospel itself, namely, that God's grace is perfected in our weakness. (*Question 4*)

After reading our memory verse once more, construct a reply to this basic question: In what, dear reader, are you boasting?

Questions for Reflection and Reply

1. Mention duties or aspects of the ministry that are *un*spectacular or *un*impressive by the world's standards.

2. Read *Heidelberg Catechism*, Lord's Day 39. In connection with our lesson, explain what it means that we 'bear patiently with their [the minister's too!] weaknesses and shortcomings, since it please God to govern us by their hand'? Where do people first learn respect for the ministers (and elders and deacons and teachers . . .) as Christ's servants?

3. Describe in some more detail (no names, please) 'the weak' in your congregation, those who have a hard time making the grade. How must we distinguish between spiritual weakness and spiritual laziness? What is the normal human response to weakness? Was Paul's 'burning with anger' a biblical pastoral response? Why (not)?

4. Discuss with fellow Bible students several 'war wounds' you have received for Christ.

Lesson 14

2 Corinthians 12:1-10

The Ecstasy and Sufficiency of Divine Grace

Memory Verse: 'And He said to me, 'My grace is sufficient for you, for
My strength is made perfect in weakness.' Therefore
most gladly I will rather boast in my infirmities, that
the power of Christ may rest upon me. . . . For when I
am weak, then I am strong.'

2 Corinthians 12:9,10c

Experiencing the height and depth of divine grace

With declared embarrassment, the apostle Paul has been 'boasting'
to the Corinthian believers of his weaknesses and sufferings. He had
temporarily adopted the style of his world-like opponents in Corinth in
order to gain a hearing among those seduced by their teaching. Irony
and sarcasm were blended in a scathing rebuke of these believers for
losing sight of the apostle's Christ-like style and grace-magnifying
leadership.

He comes, finally, to speak of receiving a sacred, indescribable
revelation, which was followed by a painful, unidentified 'thorn in the
flesh.'

The order and context of both are significant.

Far from competing with his religious opponents in a game of
spiritual one-up-manship, Paul fashions his argument to meet the fickle
loyalty of the Corinthians. If their vaunted leaders boasted of victories
and successes, Paul bragged about beatings and suffering. If the false
apostles gloried in their natural leadership abilities, this apostle exulted
in his shameful Damascus escape. But if the intruders crowed about
their private visions and revelations, where did that leave Paul? He
couldn't very well deny that he had received visions and divine revelations, for that would have been seized by his opponents to discredit
him.

So he is forced, as it were, to write about a vision so majestic and breathtaking that afterward, it took a thorn in the flesh from the Lord to keep Paul's feet on the ground.

The ecstasy of inexpressible glory (read 12:1-6)

This apostolic boasting may have been necessary because of the church's wavering loyalty, but certainly not for Paul's own psychological or spiritual well-being. So uninterested is he in himself, that he describes his vision in the third person singular!

Three clues lead us to see that Paul is the subject of this vision. First, he admits in verse 6 that were he to boast about this experience, it would not be an empty bragging, but grounded in truth. It had really happened to him! Then, in verse 7 the apostle ties the vision together with his subsequent, but related, thorn in the flesh. And third, if Paul was not the subject of the vision, his argument against the false apostles would have missed the target. Speaking about another person's vision wouldn't have raised Paul's stock in their eyes!

Why, then, does he describe his experience in the third person? Because he finds spiritual bragging so distasteful that he retells the experience impersonally, anonymously.

He writes of 'a man in Christ' (note the humility: not apostle, but ordinary Christian) to whom three things had happened fourteen years earlier (about A.D. 44).

'The third heaven' and 'Paradise'

First, he was 'caught up to the third heaven' (verse 2), 'caught up into Paradise' (verse 4). Here he heard 'inexpressible words, which it is not lawful for a man to utter' (verse 4).

Paul may have had in mind the ancient idea of heaven as three levels. The first consisted of the clouds, the second of the stars, and the third of God's spiritual dwelling. Calvin's explanation, that Paul employs the number three as symbolic of what is highest and most perfect, makes good sense.

The term 'Paradise' occurs three times in the New Testament: Luke 23:43, where Christ says to the repentant thief on the cross, 'Today you will be with me in Paradise'; our present passage; and Revelation 2:7, 'To him who overcomes I will give to eat from the tree of life, which is in the midst of the Paradise of God.' Each of these is referring to the same place, namely, the very presence of Christ Himself. Here too is the dwelling of those who have died in Christ.

In or out of the body?

Paul knows *that* he'd been translated immediately into the presence of his Savior, but *how* he was brought there, he doesn't know. Did he ascend like Enoch, body and all? Or did he encounter Christ simply as a disembodied spirit, temporarily leaving his body behind? Apparently, the answer to this question was not important, for him or us.

Inexpressible words, prohibited talk

What the apostle heard in Christ's presence is described further with two important qualifications.

The words were inexpressible. The revelation he received was incapable of translation into human words and terminology. As when one would describe the principles of electricity to an isolated tribesman in South America, here too one can only grope and fumble for word pictures (metaphors and similes) and hand pictures (gestures).

Even if it could have been communicated, this revelation was so sacred and personal, kept between the apostle and his God, upon divine orders. It was intended only for Paul, with a view to his singular apostolic suffering and service.

Why, then, does he speak of it here, almost tempting us, as it were, to inquire speculatively into its content? To remind the church, says Calvin, to be content with the limits of our knowledge, not seeking to know what the Lord has not revealed. And further, that we may be encouraged with the light of heaven's glory that does break through here, with the glimpse of inexpressible beauty and perfection to which we, now, are being called and for which we, now, are being prepared.

Again, the apostle wishes to avoid any strutting, any gloating about himself (verse 5). His glorying in the indescribable experience of fourteen years ago is a boasting in truth (verse 6a), not in himself.

So he stops, lest he go too far. He tells no more, lest his readers esteem him too highly, lest their opinion of him expand beyond what is warranted by his words and actions (verse 6b). Not his personal experiences, but his apostolic conduct must form the basis of their judgment of him. This is a helpful principle for our own day: 'No matter how spectacular the private claim, no matter how esoteric the putative vision, it cannot displace conduct and speech as more reliable indicators of how closely anyone follows Christ' (Carson). (*Questions 1 and 2*)

Grace sufficient for suffering (read 12:7-10)

Once again we, along with the Corinthians, are given some, but not all, the information. *That* the apostle suffered a 'thorn in the flesh' is plain; *what* that thorn was nobody knows.

Several facts about it are certain, however. This thorn was not a birth defect, or a character fault, that had afflicted the apostle before his heavenly revelations. It was given him *afterward.* Also, in view of his repeated prayers for its removal, the thorn must have proved quite painful, and perhaps even embarrassing, to Paul.

Most striking is the description of the thorn as 'a messenger of Satan to torment me' (verse 7). We immediately think of Job, torment- ed by Satan at God's invitation! Here too, though Satan may have been the agent, God was the superintendent. It was His purpose, not Satan's, to keep the apostle from becoming conceited. (*Question 3*)

Notice how direct and first-person Paul has become, after telling of his most exalted vision with third-person modesty. In detailing his ecstatic experience of divine grace, he directs attention away from himself; but when describing his weakness, he directs attention to the personal enjoyment of sufficient grace. Surely he has learned the 'lesson of the thorn!'

So severe was his affliction that the apostle pleaded with the Lord no fewer than three times, not with quick little prayers, but with intense intercession. He asked for the thorn's removal. And how did the Lord respond? 'My grace is sufficient for you, for my strength is made perfect in weakness' (verse 9a).

What kind of answer to prayer is this?

Calvin helps us here by distinguishing between *ends* and *means* in prayer. Paul imagined that the *end* he desired (relief from the thorn) was attainable only *by means of* its removal. The Lord showed him another means: divine grace sufficient to compensate for his weakness.

This was no new idea for the apostle, for in his earlier epistle to the Corinthians he had issued this warning against apostasy through spiritu- al seduction: 'No temptation has overtaken you except such as is common to man; but God is faithful, who will not allow you to be tempted beyond what you are able, but with the temptation will also make the way of escape, that you may be able to endure it' (1 Cor. 10:13). *Endurance by grace is the pathway of escape!*

The lesson was learned, as we read in verse 9b: 'Therefore most gladly I will rather boast in my infirmities, that the power of Christ may rest upon me.' His weakness had become the occasion for Christ to manifest His power. The lesson is applied and expanded in verse 10: 'Therefore I take pleasure in infirmities, in reproaches, in needs, in persecutions, in distresses, for Christ's sake. For when I am weak, then I am strong.'

Ah, those three words, *'for Christ's sake,'* sanctify the apostle's suffering, justify his pain and affliction. Even the thorn is bearable *for Christ's sake.*

There's something unique, almost inexplicable, about this kind of suffering. In our day of instant answers and quick fixes, *endurance* has become relegated almost exclusively to athletics. Pills, painkillers, insurance policies and retirement plans all help us 'get through' our afflictions. None is wrong in itself. But the church father Chrysostom (A.D. 345-407) had it right when he reminded ancient believers 'how great is the advantage of affliction; for now indeed that we are in the enjoyment of peace we have become supine and lax, and have filled the Church with countless evils; but when we were persecuted we were more soberminded and more earnest and more ready for church attendance and for hearing.' (*Question 4*)

Questions for Reflection and Reply

1. Who claim nowadays to have visions and private revelation from God? Does God continue to reveal Himself this way? Defend your answer from the Bible.

2. What can we learn from the apostle's *modesty* regarding his intense spiritual experience? Under what conditions should we tell others about our spiritual experiences? When does this kind of 'sharing' become 'bragging'?

3. How does this combination of Satan's strategy and God's oversight help us deal with disease, death, accidents, oppression, and so forth?

4. If you are a believer, describe how you are suffering *for Christ's sake.* What are some normal, but unbiblical, responses to persecution? When we suffer, should we pray for God to remove the 'thorn,' as the apostle did? Why (not)?

Lesson 15

2 Corinthians 12:11-21

Edified toward Congregational Repentance

Memory Verse: 'But we do all things, beloved, for your edification.'
2 Corinthians 12:19c

Congregational silence criticized (read 12:11-13)

Throughout this letter, the apostle Paul has been building a case
against false apostles who had crept into the Corinthian church to sow
seeds of heresy and immorality. Unfortunately, the believers in Corinth
had been taken in by the leadership style and blandishments of these
'super apostles.'

Until this point, Paul has used mild irony and sarcasm, soft rebuke
and gentle admonition.

In the passage we are studying in this lesson, we see him taking off
the gloves. Writing with breathtaking bluntness, he boxes the congregation's ears, so to speak, until they are red with embarrassment for
complying so easily with the seductions of false leaders.

In contrast to the intruders, Paul had avoided boasting about
himself as long as possible, until finally he erupted with the exuberant
confession, 'Therefore most gladly I will rather boast in my infirmities,
that the power of Christ may rest upon me' (2 Cor. 12:9b). Boasting in
his weakness, in his embarrassment and sufferings, became this apostle's
mark of distinction.

Paul would rather have refrained from boasting, but the Corinthians
compelled him to open his mouth. How? By their silence.

Rather than defending the apostle's message and manner among
them, they had kept their collective mouth shut, giving the false apostles free reign in criticizing Paul and his gospel. The church should
have commended him by defending his capacities as a servant of Jesus
Christ. His preaching had been confirmed with powerful signs, miracles
and wonders—what more did they need? These miraculous signs were
done 'with all perseverance' (verse 12), pointing back to those lists of

Paul's persecutions and afflictions which he considered glorious (11:22-33; 12:7-10). The Corinthians were ashamed of their spiritual father, the apostle Paul. Ashamed of his meekness (10:1), his modest rhetorical abilities (11:6), and his reticence in boasting about spiritual experiences (12:1-10). They had wanted signs but no suffering, power instead of persecution, victory without endurance.

But this congregation had nothing to be ashamed about (verse 13), for the display of divine power among them was in no way inferior to that shown among other congregations.

True, there was one detail wherein the Corinthians were inferior to other churches: the apostle had refused their financial support. 'Forgive me this wrong!' the apostle pleads with biting sarcasm. The Corinthians couldn't stand it that the apostle had refused to place himself in their debt by depending on them for support. That's what all 'normal' preachers of that day did. People expected to be exploited financially, to be 'used' by charismatic leaders. Such a relationship had mutual benefits: the leader had his 'paying' (that is: adoring) followers, and the people could brag about their 'bought-and-paid-for' minister. *(Question 1)*

The apostle had written them earlier about his right to financial support (1 Cor. 9), but indicated that for the sake of the gospel he had renounced that right. In this way, Paul was 'different' from his contemporaries—and the congregation didn't appreciate his oddness! Because the Corinthians were equating a non-essential right to financial support with a necessary qualification for being an apostle, Paul failed their test.

Pastoral sacrifice in pursuit of souls (read 12:14-16a)

When Paul arrives in Corinth for his third visit, he has no intention of changing his pastoral policy on this score. He will not be a burden to them, in order the better to show them his real motive: 'I do not seek yours, but you' (verse 14). He's not after their possessions, their bank accounts or religious pay-offs, but their *souls!*

We must be careful to understand his supporting illustration in its context: 'For the children ought not to lay up for the parents, but the parents for the children' (verse 14). From other passages we learn more about family responsibilities (1 Tim. 5:8), and also that other apostles *did* have the right to be supported by their 'children' (1 Cor. 9:3-14). Here the point is that the apostle Paul resembles a parent who desires to bring children to maturity and independence, rather than to exploit them by living off their wealth.

Like any faithful parent, the apostle is gladly willing to spend (his own resources) and be spent (sacrificing his very self) to bring these believers to maturity. But, if that be true, will the Corinthians respond with proportionate love? Will they demonstrate gratitude toward the one who has led them into the green pastures of the gospel? Such thankfulness is much more than a courtesy; 'it is simultaneously a powerful antidote to bitterness and malice, and potent acknowledgement that we stand by grace' (Carson).

No matter what the Corinthian response will be, the apostle's policy of self-sacrifice will continue. Paul will not adopt the standards employed by false leaders and by believers who naively follow them. For he is in pursuit of souls, not selfish gain. (*Question 2*)

Caught in a contradiction? (read 12:16b-19)

Paul refused to rely on the Corinthians for financial support. Yet, he had dispatched emissaries to canvas the congregation for financial contributions on behalf of the Jerusalem church (2 Cor. 9). It might well be that someone started the rumor that Paul was in fact using these donated funds to line his own pockets.

The apostolic self-defense goes to the heart of the matter: Paul had sent Titus and probably either Luke or Barnabas (cf. 8:16,18), whose methods and style had not exploited the Corinthians. Rather, these delegates had acted in the same spirit and pattern of the apostle who sent them.

Thus, it was not the apostle, but the congregation, who was caught in a contradiction. The church's scurrilous and unspiritual suspicions of the apostle, her silent complicity in the face of public rumor and reproach, rendered her guilty along with the false apostles.

The beginning of verse 19 can be translated as either a question ('Have you been thinking all along that we have been defending ourselves to you?') or a blunt declaration ('You have been thinking all along . . .'). In both cases, the effect is the same: Paul is aware of the Corinthians' mental reservations concerning his explanations. His response ought to put them to shame. He speaks before God in Christ. There is no higher Witness on his side, no greater Judge of his motives.

Just what is his motive? *'We do all things, beloved, for your edification'* (verse 19c). Building them up by fortifying faith and establishing virtue was the goal of Paul's ministry, the aim of his leadership methods. Not self-service, but soul-seeking. Not exploiting church members, but spending himself for their sake. Let every (would-be) church leader understand that *the gospel ministry is not a professional career, but a pastoral calling.*

The apostle avoids a trap that catches so many pastors, when their defense of the truth slips into self-defense, when they identify the congregation's well-being with their own. By contrast, what Christ's church needs today, more than anything else, is *a sacrificial ministry.* Pastors who demonstrate self-denial are, in reality, walking sermons that lend credibility to Sunday's homilies.

'We do *all things,*' writes the apostle—adding his affectionate address, 'beloved'—'for your edification.' Imagine what would become of the Christian ministry if all pastors engraved this motive upon their hearts, and called it to mind at the outset of every hospital call, at the opening of every sermon, every church meeting, and every salary discussion!

Concern about unmet expectations (read 12:20-21)

One of Paul's reasons for writing this epistle is to lay bare the kind of expectations held by both the apostle and the congregation for each other. If necessary, he wished to correct them, to reform them according to righteousness.

In verse 20, he admits his fear that the Corinthians might not exhibit the kind of godliness he desires. From 1 Corinthians we learn about the carnal sins that dragged the congregation down, about the divisive spirit that sapped her energy.

But notice *why* Paul fears this: 'lest, when I come again, my God will humble me among you, and I shall mourn for many who have sinned before and have not repented . . .' (verse 20). Repented from what? From sins of sexual immorality. Back in those days, 'promiscuity' and 'Corinth' were as synonymous as 'Detroit' and 'automobiles' are today. Paul remembers the Corinthians' background, and fears that his next visit to Corinth will cause him grief over their impenitent carnality.

We must be sure to grasp the connection, presented here, between the church's carnal expectations regarding ministerial leadership, and the likely companion of a carnal lifestyle. Doctrine determines morality, and the Corinthian standards for leadership are the soil in which sexual sins thrive. 'When a church or a denomination is characterized by such [doctrinal and spiritual] sins, it will not be long before it is also characterized by the grosser forms of immorality' (Carson). *Undisciplined theology and spirituality lead to undisciplined morality.* Replacing communal restraint with the values of worldly arrogance will set the church up for a disastrous fall.

But that is not the only concern expressed here by the apostle. He fears that if his visit should uncover impenitence in the congregation, God will humble *him* in the presence of the church. By means of this formulation, pastor Paul conveys a deep sense of responsibility for the maturity level of the Corinthian church. So deeply responsible, in fact, that *their* immaturity he considers to be *his* failure! He's not the kind of pastor who 'washes his hands' of the situation, saying in effect, 'Well, I've done all I could; now it's on your head.' This pastor is simply unable to discipline with dry eyes, with the cool aloofness of the professional. Just as a parent ought to feel humbled by a child's rebellion, sensing a share of the responsibility, so the apostle Paul expects to be humbled if the Corinthians remain impenitent. (*Question 3*)

Recall, as we come to the end of our lesson, that the apostle explained his ministerial motive this way: 'But we do all things, beloved, for your edification.' 'All things' includes this portion of 2 Corinthians too! His blunt rebukes and biting sarcasm are aimed at building up the Corinthian believers—all believers!—in obedient faith. Look at yourself, whether pastor or pewsitter, and examine your expectations and standards for ministerial leadership in the church. What *is* the church, anyway? Why do *you* belong to the church, anyway? As pastor or parishioner, what do you want out of what people nowadays call 'religion'? (*Question 4*)

Fundamental questions, that may just lead us to fundamental repentance!

Questions for Reflection and Reply

1. Today people refer to the practice of a minister supporting himself as a 'tentmaking' ministry. In the light of the lesson, mention some advantages of a tentmaking ministry, in contrast to a ministry that depends on congregational support—two benefits for the minister and two for the church.

2. Illustrate how a minister in pursuit of souls will do the following differently than one interested in selfish gain:

    • teach catechism

    • make pastoral calls

    • pastor the elderly

    • preach

    • pray

3. Should parents feel responsible for the conduct of their children? Was Paul correct, or just overly sensitive, in feeling responsible for the level of spiritual maturity in Corinth? Why?

4. Mention several ways in which the apostle Paul's teaching in this lesson has 'edified' or built you up in faith and obedience.

Lesson 16

2 Corinthians 13:1-14

Aiming for Congregational Maturity

Memory Verse: 'Examine yourselves as to whether you are in the faith. Prove yourselves. Do you not know yourselves, that Jesus Christ is in you?—unless you are disqualified.'

2 Corinthians 13:5

Christ's spokesman warns of impending discipline (read 13:1-4)

We have come, now, to the last chapter of 2 Corinthians. With tears born of pastoral anguish, Paul has been pleading with them to wake up, to recognize the true character of gospel-servanthood, and to turn away from false apostles with their human standards of leadership and influence.

One of the purposes of this letter has been to announce his third visit (see 12:14; 13:1), when the apostle would surely apply discipline within the congregation. This discipline would be biblical, carefully following the prescriptions for fairness laid down in the Old Testament, rules that have never been set aside. 'By the mouth of two or three witnesses every word shall be established,' he warns, quoting Deuteronomy 19:15.

His threat of impending discipline has been issued before, and here he sounds it again. The substance of his warning is this: 'If I come again, I will not spare.'

Why this bluntness, this pointed announcement? Because the Corinthians were demanding from Paul proof that Christ was speaking through him. Since they preferred the false leaders' displays of rhetorical power and fashionable leadership, they had misjudged the apostle's gentleness and meekness as being nothing but weakness. So, if it's power they want, wait until Paul visits Corinth for a third time, when he may be forced to show the power of Christ's wrath against their continuing sin.

The Corinthians' quarrel, after all, was not with Paul, but with

Christ, his Sender. But He is the risen and exalted Christ, endowed with all authority in heaven and on earth, the omnipotent Ruler sitting at the Father's right hand.

And yet, lest they misunderstand this appeal to Christ's power, the apostle paints a stunning portrait of how, in Christ, weakness and power are related: 'For though He was crucified in weakness, yet He lives by the power of God' (13:4a).

The 'weakness' in which Christ was crucified was the weakness of *self-denial*. It was the weakness spoken of elsewhere as Christ humbling Himself, emptying Himself, taking the form of a servant, becoming obedient to the Father's will all the way to the cross (Phil. 2:5-9). But the weakness of the cross was not the last word, for it was swallowed up by power—the power of resurrection. The crucifixion and resurrection, the cross and the crown, belong together; the one cannot be understood without the other.

For Christ, weakness was not the absence of power, but its prerequisite. This power, moreover, was not the achievement earned through self-assertion, but the reward for self-sacrifice. (*Question 1*)

Next, Paul employs this combination and manifestation of weakness and power as a model for Christians, especially apostles and their ministerial successors: 'For we also are weak in Him, but we shall live with Him by the power of God toward you' (13:4b). Notice that weakness is the apostle's *current* condition, whereas power is the *future* prospect. Voluntary self-denial, in the ministry and in the Christian life, is the route toward divine empowerment.

The congregation summoned to self-examination (read 13:5-6)

The prospect of Paul's announced third visit, along with the possibility of stern church discipline, leads to the sober summons which serves as our memory verse for this lesson: 'Examine yourselves as to whether you are in the faith. Prove yourselves. Do you not know yourselves, that Jesus Christ is in you?—unless you are disqualified' (13:5).

For so long now these church members had been examining Paul's apostolic credentials and claims, comparing them to those of the false apostles. Now it's time to turn the searchlight around on themselves. And what a fundamental challenge is put to them by the apostle: 'See whether you are in the faith.' See if you're really Christians!

Why this test of self-knowledge? Well, if they know Jesus Christ to be 'in themselves,' then they must also know that Paul is the one who proclaimed Christ to them. These Corinthian Christians will then recognize themselves as Paul's letter of commendation (see 3:2), as the seal of his divinely given apostleship. To these believers Paul's appeal is logical and simple: *the genuineness of their position in Christ stands or falls with the genuineness of his authority as Christ's apostle.*

This logic helps explain verse 6: 'But I trust that you will know that we are not disqualified.' If the Corinthians pass the test, then the man who first led them into grace cannot be quite as worthless as some have been claiming. He too must be given a passing grade when his ministry among them is judged by proper standards of leadership. If they fail the test, then, true enough, Paul will be humiliated—but they will be in no position to point a critical finger at him or anyone else.

This is quite an interesting rejoinder by the apostle, isn't it? To prepare them for his visit, he calls his Corinthian critics to look carefully, not at his message or his manner, nor those of his rivals, but *at themselves*, at their Christian experience and position in Christ. Humanly speaking, whom do they have to thank for this? Why, the apostle Paul, of course!

A pastor's prayer for congregational maturity (read 13:7-10)

The apostle's prayers deserve a study all by themselves. Often at the beginning of his letters, occasionally at the end, and even sandwiched in the middle, these prayers throb with a pastor's heartbeat. (*Question 2*)

His prayer for the Corinthians captures everything he's been writing: 'Now I pray to God that you do no evil, not that we should appear approved, but that you should do what is honorable, though we may seem disqualified' (verse 7). Paul prays not for his own vindication, but for their preservation from sin. Once more he urges the repentance of those who, by life or teaching, are contradicting the gospel.

What is his motive? Not that he, Paul, might look good, but that the Corinthians might turn away from error, and thereby avert the apostle's stern discipline, and perhaps even make him look foolish for such intense concern.

In verse 8 the apostle seems to be saying that if he should find, upon arrival in Corinth, humble repentance and godly sorrow, any display of apostolic authority through discipline would work against the truth of the gospel. Only in the face of continued disobedience is that disciplining authority necessary.

In this context, therefore, 'weakness' would delight the apostle. That is, if his threatened discipline were 'neutralized' by their repentance (which would demonstrate their 'strength'), so that his threat would fall to the ground unenforced, why, he would rejoice!

What genuine pastoral humility is expressed in Paul's simple petition: 'And this also we pray, that you may be made complete' (verse 9b). The congregation's perfection, maturity, and completeness—these are the single goal of ministerial leadership, of preaching and discipline. Such leadership rises above retaliation, refuses to take cheap shots at the congregation, and sets aside all questions of personal security and promotion. (*Question 3*)

But this apostolic tenderness is also realistic. Although Paul hopes that his letter will produce good results, he is prepared to use his Lord-given authority if those results are not forthcoming. That authority *can* destroy, if the Corinthian church should prove to be a false church and the rot of unbelief requires removal. But even that destruction serves the further aim of edification, of rebuilding something better. The choice rests with the Corinthians themselves, as to how the apostle's authority will need to be used among them.

Till we meet again (read 13:11-14)

Farewells can often be painful. But the lingering wishes of a loving 'good bye' can last for a long time.

The pastoral farewell of this epistle contains four crisp exhortations.

The first is: 'Become complete.' Aim for perfection. Paul picks up the word he used in verse 9, the single aim of his prayer for the Corinthians: 'that you may be made complete.' (*Question 4*)

The second encouragement is: 'Be of good comfort'—turning the reader back to the very first verses of this epistle (read 1:3-7).

A third injunction follows: 'Be of one mind,' calling these believers to work hard at coming to agreement, to unity of thought and confession, in order to live out of that oneness.

Finally, the apostle urges the Corinthians to 'live in peace.' The opposite of peace is polarization, which sadly generates sinful slander, jealousy and backbiting. Peace comes through reconciliation, the reconciliation described so beautifully earlier in 5:18-21.

How shall they heed these admonitions? The apostle cements his farewell with this blessing: 'and the God of love and peace will be with you' (verse 11b). The presence of God, whose character and gifts are best described with the words 'love' and 'peace,' is both the source and condition for interpersonal harmony in the church.

Such harmony is given visible expression through the ancient custom of greeting with a kiss. Here, Paul exhorts church members of that day to exchange a *holy* kiss (for us: a holy handshake). Why 'holy'? Because what is symbolized by a handshake between Christians—namely, unity at the foot of the cross—is sacred, too sacred to play around with.

What an encouragement it is for the apostle to extend greetings from 'all the saints' (verse 13). It is true that the means of grace, gospel preaching and the holy sacraments, are given to local churches for bringing people to faith or strengthening existing faith. But the scope of divine redemption extends beyond the city limits.

The apostle's final benediction constitutes his closing prayer, his concluding advice for the Corinthian church situation—and for ours: 'The grace of the Lord Jesus Christ, the love of God, and the communion of the Holy Spirit be with you all. Amen' (verse 14). *The grace of the Lord Jesus Christ* is the source and example of self-denial; *the love of God the Father* provides the antidote to jealousy and unholy competition; and *the communion of the Holy Spirit* bestows the spiritual power for overcoming petty quarrels and for living together in love.

This trinitarian benediction, with which many pastors conclude divine worship, proclaims an order of heavenly blessing with a climax and crescendo: *grace . . . love . . . communion.* Grace finds expression in love and communion, and is their prerequisite for enjoyment. Divine love is the spark that ignites grace to produce the warmth of spiritual fellowship.

The apostle is ready, now, to end his letter. His familiar 'amen' serves as a final declaration of pastoral confidence that his prayers and pleadings will bear fruit. That confidence roots not in his person or pen, but in his Sender and Savior. As we end our study of this blessed epistle, may we all acknowledge the supremacy of this Savior, whose style and sacrifice ought to set the tone for pastoral leadership and congregational conduct alike. May God's power truly be magnified in all our weakness! (*Question 5*)

Questions for Reflection and Reply

1. Reread that paragraph, and reflect on why Jesus Christ looks so foolish to the world.

2. Find three prayers of the apostle Paul in other letters. Summarize the theme of each, and explain how they relate to the rest of the letter in which each prayer is found.

3. Sometimes ministers 'use' congregational prayers to 'get at' church members or to 'preach' another sermon. What biblical advice would you offer a pastor so that congregational or pastoral prayers may be genuine worship for church members?

4. Notice the *passive* voice in verse 9b ('be made complete') and the *active* voice in verse 11 ('become complete'). How does this illustrate divine sovereignty and human responsibility in redemption? What does the phrase 'ora et labora' mean, and how is it illustrated by these verses?

5. Summarize the basic theme and several lessons you have learned from your study of this epistle.